T5-ANY-232

A Quick but Important Note

Please Read:

AS THE READER YOU FULLY AGREE THAT YOU ARE SOLELY RESPONSIBLE FOR KNOWING AND OBEYING THE LAWS OF YOUR COMMUNITY OR ANY COMMUNITY YOU HAPPEN TO VISIT WHERE THIS INFORMATION COULD BE PUT INTO PLACE OR TAKEN INTO USE.

AND AS THE READER, YOU ALSO AGREE THAT THE AUTHOR "RAY WEST" OR ANYONE ACCOSSIATED WITH HIS BUSINESS IS NOT RESPONSIBLE FOR THE WAY THIS INFORMATION IS PUT INTO USE.

Free bonus gifts below...

Free Bonus Gifts can be accessed at the private URL below
Go to...
http://www.rayscorner.com/free-gifts.html

If you have difficulty reaching the page, please wait, or call 804-897-7250

Welcome Friend

Welcome to the world of adult video. I am very pleased you decided to purchase this rare publication. This book represents many years of personal experience. For a long time I debated about bringing my information public. Since many things have changed in my life, I have decided to share what I know.

In this book, I am going to go over many topics concerning your adult video start-up. My job is to help you along this exciting path. Since this business is geared towards working with attractive women, it's a path worth traveling.

This industry alone grossed well over several billion dollars last year. This figure continues to grow rapidly. The market potential is tremendous. For many video stores, this industry keeps them in business. It's an industry that will be around for a very long time. A common phrase is "if a nuclear war ever broke out, the only thing left would be cock roaches and the adult industry".

I have also included a number of questions throughout the guide that were asked of me throughout my career. I will include these same questions, with my answers.

Everything written in this book is <u>directly written</u>. Most publications today are over fabricated, with every major detail grouped together. This guide was written to unfold like a conversation. I prefer to write with my heart and not with the aid of a "Harvard" textbook. Each major topic of your soon-to-be adult video business is expressed continually throughout the entire book. I may mention a key point in the beginning, then I may talk more about it in the middle and so on. I personally think it makes the reading much easier. My purpose is to talk to you. I am strongly against forcing words on a page. My purpose was to write something that was easy and fun to read. I vowed to myself if I was ever going to write this book, I would make it enjoyable.

My Personal Goal

My personal goal is to get you on your way to personal and financial freedom. For reasons discussed later, I was able to retire from this business very successful. I started 12 years ago, and I have not answered to any supervisor or boss since. I was able to drive my first Mercedes Benz at 21 years of age. I was also able to visit many parts of the world three or four times a year, and open a second office in Los Angeles. Now, my purpose is not to brag. I just want to give you an idea of what's possible.

I will never forget the day, when I clocked out at my regular job 12 years ago. It's a feeling of being born again. And I want to share that feeling with you.

I have supported myself with many pleasures both financially and personally. I hope this guide helps you with many pleasures that lay ahead in the world of adult video. I also look forward and pray for that feeling to shine even brighter once it comes.

Let's begin!

Ray West

well done. The first scene focuses on areas of the woman like the ankle and legs. Then the camera zooms on to her face. The scene works you up slowly, giving you a little dose of anticipation at a time. The woman talks about herself, hobbies and what not. She then stands up with her long dark hair stretching to the small of her back. Her legs are well-shaped within tight slacks. You get to see her disrobe slowly and pose on the bed with the action following. I saw that film 9 years ago, and I still continue to tell people about it. That type of film in my opinion is much better than watching drunken bimbos with beer bellies fall all over the place. When I was 18 that might have turned me on but that's really pushing it.

With the films I produced in the past, such as the "One For the Road" series, I detailed every camera angle to the fullest for the viewers enjoyment. I try to make the most out of every shot. I like to tease the viewer with the camera motions. To keep things exciting. Exploring every scene to it's fullest before moving on to the next. I myself love focusing on a woman's legs and face before moving on to other areas of interest. Also, I always make it a priority to introduce the woman/actress to the audience. This makes the scene more personal and invites the audience to join the fantasy. Allowing her personality to bloom in front of my viewers carries the fantasy much further.

Getting turned on takes on many different angles. To hit on each angle and display them to the fullest is a true masterpiece of work. This all leads to making the woman feel comfortable with her inhibitions left behind. The biggest turn on is watching this process unfold slowly. Everyone wins with this type of film work. The actress gets turned on, the viewer, and of course myself. It's very difficult to fake sexual pleasure. The slow worked up effect is the honest effect. A good example would be riding a rollercoaster. When you're going up that first hill, the anticipation is exhilarating. Same goes for adult entertainment. Your job is to give the viewer the ride of his or her life. Essentially you are the builder of that roller coaster. You have to plan the angles and hills, then test them to see how they work. **There are many cheap carnivals but very few Six Flag's.**

How did you find the Talent?

Having the best talent for your video is the first major step for creating a quality picture. **The right kind of talent is attractive talent.** Having attractive natural looking women in your movies will produce many sales. Your search at times can be a difficult process. Having the right cast could take longer than expected, but by any means it's extremely important.

When I had the first idea to start, I had no idea where to start my search. I honestly couldn't see myself walking up to some woman and asking her to star in a sex film. So, I thought about going to the local topless bars to see what I could do there. That's where I ended up finding my first cast member.

Before I ventured out, I printed up some business cards with my phone number and name. I decided to go on a weeknight to avoid any large crowds. Upon my arrival I settled myself at a nearby table close to the stage. After ordering a drink, I sat back and was surprised at the number of girls working that night. Usually on weekdays there's only a handful of girls working, but that night if I remember correctly, I saw at least 10. At this point I was still too nervous to start handing out cards to some of the girls passing me by. I ordered another drink. After 30 minutes of my arrival, a very friendly dancer came and sat down next to me. She introduced herself as Simone. She had long dark hair and stood about 5'7". She was very attractive. She had everything I was looking for.

After she gave me a quick lap dance, I asked her if she would like to join me at the bar. She agreed.

Thereafter, we started having a good conversation. I remember talking about the new layout of the club and how they had added another stage. After talking for a few minutes, she asked me if I came to the club alone. I told her yes, and that I was looking for girls for an upcoming project I had in mind. She smiled, and asked me what kind of project? I told her straight out that I was going to make an adult film. To my surprise, she didn't seem that fazed. She then told me, how her and her ex-boyfriend use to film themselves together. I quickly noticed the word "ex-boyfriend". Was she now single? She happily answered yes. **This was sounding good.**

Later on, I offered her my business card, for her phone number in return. She happily agreed. Right away this indicated a possible interest. I was doing my job.

The following day I decided to give Simone a call. Once in contact, I told her how much I enjoyed her company the night before.

After 15 minutes of talking, I told her straight out how perfect she would be for my upcoming film. She told me she wasn't sure. I then asked her to meet me somewhere for a casual drink to discuss further. After, asking a few more times, she agreed.

Halfway through the meeting I tried my best to stay relaxed since this was completely new for me. I started describing her the picture I was going to make, and what I needed. She then asked, if I was going to star in the film with her? I politely asked her if that was ok. She silently said yes.

After we both discussed her billing (*I paid $175*), I now had my first cast member.

The only thing left to discuss was when & where?

We both agreed on the next weekend, at a local hotel.
Until that time, I relentlessly continued to go over possible scenes in my head. I kept picturing her in many different outfits. I kept thinking which ones I would like better.

Since Simone had nice shaped thighs, I pictured her wearing a short black executive dress with a tight white T-shirt. For shoes, I pictured black high heels with a high arch.

I called her the following night to run everything by her. She agreed to the outfit ideas, and that she had everything to put the outfit together.

With the long awaited weekend arriving, I was feeling confident but nervous at the same time. It's easy to sit in your own home and imagine yourself in the video, but this was **real**.

I also wondered about being able to perform without any problems.

Constructing a picture with many details, while trying to maintain a hard on, is not always easy.

As the meeting timed neared for filming, I quickly made my way to the hotel lobby. When she arrived, she looked very sleek and beautiful. She was wearing the exact outfit I had asked for. After approaching with a simple greeting, we decided to make our way to the room.

With the camera battery fully charged, my dream of starting my very first adult video was about to begin.

I informed Simone that I wanted her to tease the camera. Especially in the opening shots.

With Simone sitting in a nearby chair with her legs slightly arched. My camera power light came on. After briefly introducing myself, I announced proudly, that a beautiful young woman was in the presence.

I then started moving the camera picture slowly up her body, until I had a close-up of her face.

I then started asking her about sex. I asked her how often she performed it, and what sexual positions she enjoyed the most.

Afterwards, I asked her if she would like to stand up, so everyone could see her body. After she stood up, she leaned over the chair to show off her ass. I was completely speechless.

When Simone moved onto the bed, I politely asked her to remove her top. With that happening, beautiful tanned breasts emerged.

When she later removed her dress. I could not believe I was in the same room with this woman. My worries quickly went from not being able to perform, but how long I could hold out.

I was now ready to leave my mark and move in. I angled my camera on the dresser, and crawled into the bed. After getting undressed and propping myself next to her, I asked her to demonstrate how she masturbated. With her black panties off, everything was under way.

Eventually, we both worked our way into the actual sex. I must remind you, that in this business nothing is more important than safe sex. I wore a condom. Moving on….

After working different positions, I finished the scene with her giving me a blowjob. After climaxing, I can only describe the release as unimaginable. I had turned my fantasy into reality. I was extremely thrilled, to finally live my vision.

After you make your first film, you always remember it.

The story you just read was my first experience in adult films. Nobody knocked on my door and brought me into this life. I went to it <u>alone</u>. Before that first day, I was a fan, like millions of others. Now I was among the creators.

Searching Talent

Since many girls come from the topless bars, this however is not the only place to look. Some of my best female talent were college students. Thank god for higher education. In some cases they were both (students & dancers). College student by day, dancer by night. With the tuition rates for college sky rocketing, you would be surprised what some ladies are willing to do.

Also, another thing to think about is the fact many topless dancers are usually quite burned out from showing off their bodies and talents. Since they perform around large groups of men five to six nights a week, they are usually drained. College women on the other hand seemed drained on not showing their bodies often enough.

Depending where you live, it's sometimes common to see ads in local college newspapers and newsletters, offering nude modeling work. I have seen my share. Now I know, nude-modeling work is very different from adult film work. But in some cases, this is a known advertising tactic used to find women for adult films. Clear your mind for a second, and think about this....for 9 months, what environment can you consistently find young vibrant women? And what's one of their biggest needs? The answers are colleges and money. That's right "Girls Just Wanna Have Funds"!

Here's an idea you can have fun with. When you have some free time, go to a local college. Take a bright sheet of paper, find the college's bulletin board and place a simple ad like the one below. **Example only.**

SEEKING ATTRACTIVE WOMEN ONLY FOR NUDE MODELING WORK

COULD THIS BE YOU?

IF YOU FIT THIS TYPE

CALL xxxxxxxxxx

TO SPEAK WITH xxxxxxxxxxx

SPECIAL NOTE. PLEASE READ. THIS IS AN EXAMPLE ONLY. I HAVE NO WAY OF KNOWING YOUR STATES LAWS. BEFORE YOU MAKE ANY ATTEMPT TO PLACE ANY ADS. CHECK YOUR STATE AND LOCAL LAWS FIRST.

As you can tell, the example above is not meant to be overly fancy. Your message is only there to make its statement. That's it. Its purpose is to have women take notice, and call you. It's that simple. With this sample ad, you could expect an attractive quality of women to respond. A small descriptive message will go a long way.

Now your probably wondering why not just advertise "Girls Needed For Kinky Video"? Because this type of ad automatically has the word "sleaze" written all over it. Plus, you can safely bet it will be torn down. Remember, the adult industry as a whole is trying to come across more professionally. That's the difference between the best in the industry to those who carelessly spam the Internet. **Those people are about greed not pleasure. Plus, 99% of them are losing money!**

Getting back…
After you receive some callbacks from your ads; ask the women if they have ever considered doing any adult-film work. If they answer yes, then try to set up a meeting. Choose somewhere convenient and local for the both of you to meet. In the past, I've mostly met people at cafés or my office if they felt comfortable. I find that meeting someone in public makes it a lot easier when breaking the ice. First meetings can be difficult sometimes. This idea of public location helps everyone to relax. I also recommend talking about other subjects besides the offer of employment right at first. When I first meet someone who I'm considering for one of my films, I really enjoy digging in to find out more about them. I asked about their goals, family, and their dating experience. After talking about other subjects I find it much easier to discuss any sexual acts they would consider doing or not doing. Such acts would be lesbian scene work, oral, and anal to name just a few. Most women who accept the work prefer to do really anything except anal. If your movie is centered on this subject, you might have to offer a larger wage for that type of scene work.

On the other hand when you meet a woman who isn't really attractive, you have to make an effort not to hurt their feelings by letting them know they're not right for the job. When these occasions happened, I never looked forward to it. Because everyone knows the feeling of being turned down. It can hurt. Most of the time the women do understand. I've turned down many women for work, not solely based on their appearance all the time but based on wages to be paid. I have also had the challenge of narrowing down five "attractive" women, to choose only two or three for an upcoming feature. Most of the women that I talk to by phone are for the most part friendly. They are usually very excited about starting, even after they realize it's for adult film work.

Also, when I meet someone for the first time it's always during the day. Because they have no idea who I am, except by telephone and from the want ad. Having the comfort level working for you will have their confidence level enhanced on that first face to face meeting. Keep in mind again, when someone calls in reference to your ad "nude model work", make absolute **certain** you ask them if they would be interested in adult film work. If for some reason you forget to mention this, then your probably going to waste your time meeting them in person. Once someone mentions they might or would be interested in adult film work, then set the meeting up with them. That way when you go to meet, that person will already know what the job description will be. The last thing you want to do is tell them in public that you are a x-film producer, and risk them walking out on you and wasting your time. So again, when someone calls in reference to your ad, **let them know** halfway through the phone conversation that the job is for adult film work. Also, whenever you talk to someone, especially on the phone, ask them for their age. In the United States the legal age for adult film/nude work for anyone is 18. Not a day short. Also, if someone says there 18 or older ask if they have **2 forms of ID** to prove it, and ask them to bring it with him or her when you meet them in person. This will save you time and possible serious legal problems. You would be very surprised at the number of times I've had potential actresses lie about their age. I always made sure I had at least 2 ID'S to ensure legal age before I filmed my adult films. Many people will say their 18, then they will turn around and say "what I meant was, I turn 18 this fall!". Before you even turn on your camera, make absolute certain anyone starring in your film is

18 at that moment. That is the most important **law** in the adult industry. If you film anyone who is considered a minor, there could be some serious jail time. That's why it is **so important** to have at least 2 IDS from anyone starring in your films. I also recommend finding someone with a copying machine (or purchasing one), because you will have to make photocopies of all IDS and file them for your own personal/legal records. During the beginning when my budget was small, I would have the woman follow me to the local office/drugstore and use the copying machine their. After I copied her 2 IDS with her signature, that was it. It took only a couple minutes.

Make sure your answering machine is working at all hours of the night. You will receive calls from women at all hours. Especially from a college ad placed on a board or from the local campus paper. Furthermore, when you set up your answering machine make absolute certain you mention your company name along with your name at the beginning of the message. Remember that you are the business and not just the individual. Doing this makes you come across as being professional. Plus, it will make your potential actresses more comfortable from your initial first impression. With that in mind, be sure to keep calendar & notebook handy. With the amount of calls, it's real easy to lose track. Make it a habit to keep pen and paper close.

Now there will be many ladies to turn down the offer of starring in an adult film, but you will also be surprised to find a handful who will **want** to star. Obviously, this will also have to do with the wage being offered. I have had past instances where a young woman ranked #3 on a scale of 1 to 10, demanded a crazy figure of 600 dollars to star in a movie. On the same note I had a woman who could rank as high as a #9, offered to do the same movie for 125 dollars. In the world of adult video 125 dollars is a very low wage. Even for the adult video producer to offer whom is just starting out. The 200-dollar figure is quite standard for a complete segment for each actress. This also has to do with the overall appearance of the actress. I personally think if the actress is very attractive, then 200 is a good starting point and 300 would be the max. However, when you become successful, as your tapes increase in sales, 300 dollars will then appear as a low wage. It's very important to have very attractive women in your videos. This sounds like common advice, but take notice on how many adult videos today are very lacking in this area. It's very disappointing to see tapes with young women who look like they haven't slept in five days.

Another tip concerning bulletin boards. Try using the boards at the health clubs. They tend to have worked really well for me in the past. You can expect women with very nice bodies to reply. Many are ready to show it off, and then some. With the health clubs you can expect women from all areas such as the gymnasts, swimmers, tennis players, and the aerobic instructors to name just a few. Depending on the state laws concerning submission for temporary employment, this area is well worth looking into.

No matter where you live, colleges are everywhere. Whether it be community colleges or major university's. Take the time to observe their bulletin boards. If it's a large university, find out how many they have?

In the Los Angeles area you can find many ads reading nude modeling work in many adult orientated newspapers like the **L.A. Express**, which many X-film producers use to find talent. Also, believe it or not there are actual talent agencies that represent many amateur adult video actresses who use this very same form of advertising for nude model work. An example of an agency in particular is **"World Modeling"** based in Southern California. If you get a chance, check out "World Modelings" website at **www.worldmodeling.com.**

Another unique way of finding possible talent is by ways of the Internet. There are some Adult classified sites, that puts many people in contact with each other who have similar sexual interests. One such site is **adultfriendfinder.com**. I must add that this site is one of the best with its kind. This site does not charge anything but requires you to register.

Another source for online adult classified ads, is at **Excite.com** believe it or not. Excite's personal selection varies from Romance to Adult. The personal listing breaks down all 50 states and even offers other country's. Check the adult category at Excite.com for possible sources close to you.

So the decisions on choosing talent is not always simple. This is especially true when starting out, since the budget is often quite low for producing a film. Hiring talent for your videos will for the most part, be the biggest expense for putting your video together. Once you have the tape finished, **you have a solid product** ready for marketing and it belongs to no one but **YOU**!

The talent on your finished film product reflects the quality of your film. When someone visits an adult store for movies, the quality of women is what they look for first. Furthermore, when you start to promote your tape, the video store buyers & distributors will look for the same quality as well. It does amaze me though how some distributors buy lousy movies to resell (they must get them **very** cheap).

Using your Vacation to Explore Further Opportunity

When you decide to take your next vacation, you could always take your work with you. Now I know what you're thinking, "who wants to work on vacation"? Here's what I mean. Each year thousands if not millions of beautiful young women flock to many areas for spring break. Such places would be Daytona Beach, Padre Island (Texas), and Palm Springs. Would you believe how many X-film producers' travel to these locations looking for beautiful inexpensive talent? Each spring you can surely bet they are out there. From past experience it's very simple to find many willing young ladies (18+). They are also quick to settle for very low wages. Many go to the beach resorts and end up running out of money very fast. Many women go there to let loose and leave their inhibitions behind. So if you were planning a vacation, I would highly recommend taking it in the spring. I would also say Fort Lauderdale and Padre Island (Texas) remains two of the best locations. However, there are many more like Palm Springs, CA. It's very easy to spend a week at one of these locations and come back home with enough material to put two and sometimes three films together. When you arrive back home, the only thing really left is to edit and market your product. Also, with Spring Break your selection of beautiful ladies are vast and easy to locate. If you, live on the East Coast head to Florida or the shores of New Jersey (Jersey Shore). If you live in the mid-west head to Padre Island, Texas (great location). If you live on or near the West coast head for Palm Springs or Lake Havasu, Arizona.

When planning your trip, compare packages from different travel agencies. Start comparing three to four months before Spring Break (late March-early April). Finding a great deal from a travel agency is easy, especially if you plan ahead during the winter months.

Another great idea for traveling in search of talent and vacation is one of my personal favorites, Las Vegas. This town in my opinion is the capital of adult entertainment and other things as well. Once you arrive in Las Vegas, you really don't have to look far to find beautiful talent. Along Las Vegas Boulevard "The Strip", especially during the night, you can find people handing out X-rated related flyers and booklets. Believe me when I say, you will not have a hard time finding these people. They stand all along the Strip (at night) in front of major hotels and casinos handing out adult literature. This type of advertising would seem illegal to many outsiders but these individuals are practicing by the law and this form of advertising is completely legit. Also, if you decide to visit Las Vegas, pick yourself up a copy of the **Las Vegas X Press**. You can find this paper at any newsstand, 7-11, or any other convenience store. This newspaper is very similar to the LA Xpress, in which models or actresses advertise their services for adult film work. This adult newspaper is only 25 cents to purchase, and provides endless pages of beautiful potential. Definitely worth checking out.

Hotels in Vegas

In Vegas, the hotel rooms are very affordable, and these rooms are at the major resorts! I once stayed at the "Sahara" for 24 dollars per night, and this room had an outside balcony overlooking the city.

Again, taking a trip to film your work can be easier in some cases for getting your film made. Also, consider bringing a friend along and split the travel costs between the two of you. Most people would love to be a part of an adult video production (especially a friend or two). When I planned my first trip to Vegas, I actually had a hard time getting a friend to go with me. When everyone sometimes be grim, adult films offer an escape from the same sequence of reality. It takes the viewer on a sexual mind trip. To see beautiful women in erotic situations triggers strong mental and physical stimulations. You can safely bet the adult film industry will be around for some time. Many people who would never seem the type to rent/buy adult films are in fact there best customers. The billions of dollars that the industry earns each year has to be coming from somewhere.

What makes this industry so special is that it's customers come from all walks of life. People from all different races, ethnic backgrounds, white/blue collar workers, women, and basically anyone else you can think of. It's a culturally universal market. Many people from other countries abroad watch American X-rated films. They probably can't understand the language, but then again who is really listening. A funny tidbit or saying in the adult industry is that 65% of the people who watch X-rated films watch them with the volume turned down. I guess the reason behind this, is people do not want others down the hall to hear what they are really watching.

What do you think about adult film Scripts?

I myself like many others could care very less about the script. Especially since it is fabricated before filming. I prefer spontaneity. When its not fabricated, it becomes more real. I do find some from earlier films that are quite humorous. Instead of getting turned on, I laugh at some of the one liners. However, in the past and currently, I do not watch adult movies for sheer laughter. In the past, I have tried to keep everything simple and natural as can be. When something is rehearsed you can usually see it during the actual performance. Getting turned on really doesn't demand too much, but when a scene seems really fake it doesn't do the audience any good. Being spontaneous is the key. I mean who would want to write a script for a porno. First of all it can be very time consuming and having people remembering all those lines will waste all your time. When you give some direction and let people take things from there, everything will work out fine. The scenes will be fully heated and the lustful passion will be there.

How difficult is it to get actors/actresses to display full Ecstasy during filming?

As the filming progresses, this part will fall into place on it's own. I believe once the stars of the film (especially newcomers) gain further confidence in themselves, they will then be able to run wild with many sexual ideas. A lot of this confidence comes in the form of reaching that comfort zone with doing certain acts. With newcomers in the beginning, it can be quite difficult to reach that confidence level. This is true for anyone who has ever been in the adult industry. As the scene progresses further and further the confidence level becomes much smoother. This is especially true with young actresses. Many women have a great self-awareness on appearance, appearing nude for a sex scene makes it even more difficult. However, once things started rolling, I noticed many young women reached there comfort zones quite rapidly. After that point, they tend to blend through the remaining scene without any problems.

How has the adult industry changed in the Recent years?

The adult industry has gone through many phases, but still essentially the entertainment side remains 95% the same. For instance, during the 1970's adult films were mainly stories with actual plots believe it or not. There were actual writers who worked on scripts like they were trying to win the academy award.

These "70's films" were mainly and only shown in adult theatres. The VCR revolution was not yet beginning during this time. Adult theatres use to populate the United States in large numbers. During the 1970's instead of moving your films into video stores, which at the time did not really exist, you had to try and sell your film idea to the theater owners. Plus, not to mention many people did not want to go to these theaters with the fear of embarrassment. These theatres did create large profits but by all means did not get near the audience the videotape grasped. The videotape and VCR allowed people to enjoy adult entertainment in their own homes. During the 1970's this was not possible. With privacy concerns covered, the multi billion-dollar videotape industry was born. Even today, though the majority of renters/buyers are male, women are starting to make huge impacts on the consumer end. This of course is excellent news for anyone in the industry since women make up over half the total population. Plus, with more and more women supporting the industry it helps ward of any added controversy. It's always nice to have more people stand for adult film rights.

What's the biggest Controversy concerning adult films today?

Probably the biggest issue concerning adult films today is whether or not it causes someone to commit sexual crimes. Some of the so-called experts claim adult films cause people to do bodily harm to others. To tell you the truth I really do not know where these so called experts come from. I find their theories to be very far off and in the wrong direction. If all the movies from G to XXX were wiped out of existence, there would still be crimes occurring. It has nothing to do with films. It has become common and easy to blame something else besides the actual person who commits the crime. Most children do not learn their first filthy words from television; they learn them from school. There will always be influences, but to simply blame an outlet is totally off from the point. It's the parent's job to keep pornographic material away from children. Parents have to be there for there children and stop blaming other people for not doing there job. That's why laws are passed, to try and keep underage individuals from obtaining such materials. I am a strong supporter of laws of that nature. However, I do not support people attempting to abolish the industry completely. That's not the solution. I am very thankful for the first amendment. Without it, the adult industry probably would not exist among other industries, as we know it. The adult industry like any other business pays taxes to help build society in many positive ways. You will never hear that argument from anyone with opposition. The money that comes from tax dollars earned in the sex industry actually go's towards health care and government salaries to name just a few. Plus again, this industry is not just some fly by night, this industry is worth billions each year. That's a lot of tax dollars coming from this industry alone.

Another argument concerns zoning issues with video stores that carry adult films. In some counties across the U.S., zoning laws are enforced on video stores that carry adult content. This county law stipulates any video store with X-rated material to be x amount in distance from any school or shopping center. Many areas are starting to enforce this law. Again, this law is mainly a local county law instead of a federal law. Furthermore, I actually agree on some parts of this law. I wouldn't agree to have an X-rated store directly next to a school. However, to limit distances based on miles I think is going a little to far. You never hear anyone complain about having a bar to close? It's always smoking and x-films that get the bad wrap. Drunk driving actually kills more young people than anything else. Thankfully that statistic has decreased.

What areas Constitute the Main Artery of adult Film/Video production?

Adult films are made practically anywhere and come from all areas of the world. However, if there were one place that made the biggest impact in terms of adult output it would be Southern California. To be exact it would be the San Fernando Valley located north of Los Angeles. As a former resident of Los Angeles, I could not agree more. This area is the central artery of the adult industry. More X-rated movies are produced there than anywhere else on the globe. Plus, more films are manufactured (packaged) and distributed from this area as well. This is true since many major distributors are based there. Many top X-rated production companies are there to. Such companies include Vivid, Wicked, and VCA. The valley itself incorporates many smaller towns or cities within. Cities such as Van Nuys, Canoga Park, Reseda, and Pacoima to name just a few. In fact if the valley itself were separated from Los Angeles with all the towns inside combined, it would be the sixth largest city in the U.S. However, if you ever get a chance to visit there someday, you will notice how plain the area looks. One would never guess it to be "Porn Valley" as it is commonly referred. Many of the film studios are well hidden and take place in ordinary buildings. From the outside you would never know. A lot of filming also takes place in rented homes or mansions. This is quite popular with many production companies. In the long run with the number of films produced, it ends up saving money.

However, as we will discuss later, you will not need to go that far to get everything rolling in the right direction.

How did you find the Motivation to get up and start this type of Business?

After awhile, I got real tired of living a life full of boredom and less means. This misery consisted of working endless jobs that proved to be more of a nightmare. I was tired of working hard jobs for less pay in return. All of my friends seemed to be in the same situation, but they seemed hopeless to make any effort to get out. I on the other hand was willing to try something new to better my life and myself. Which is not easy when it goes from talking about it to actually doing it. Talking about it was the easy part. Doing it took some digging. The biggest part of the digging was believing I could make something happen. Believing in myself at first was a difficult obstacle. It's real easy to tell someone you believe in yourself but to actually have full faith, took some work for me. In the very beginning, I had nothing to fall back on in terms of success. That's why starting is so hard. It's easy when you have results to base progress, but starting out offers more surprises. This could be good/bad or both. Sometimes the easiest tasks in the world seem like the most difficult or unattainable. I was really surprised in my early journey with adult films, to realize everything was much better than anticipated. I was very shocked with the quick results and early earning potential. I used to be the type of person to always expect the worst. After those early days, I was starting to change my mental habits. I was not expecting the worse anymore; I was expecting the best. My belief in accomplishing my goals (business/personal) was taking more shape with each passing day. Without the adult industry I would not enjoy the financial/personal freedom I enjoy today. I have not answered to any boss/supervisor in many years thanks to the adult industry as a whole. I am extremely thankful to take many exotic vacations without having to ask someone permission for vacation time. I really cannot understand how most people in today's world are so quick to settle for less. Nothing is written in stone saying you must work a crappy job for 30 years. My favorite quote is "why does someone value themselves in pennies, when they are worth a kings ransom".

Now every job of course has its ups and downs but what I mean by crappy is exactly what it says. I strongly live by the old motto "you only live once". Very true saying. You will never see a U-haul at a funeral. My thought during my early days was " I have to find a way out of this grim day to day reality". People can only take so much before they realize something has to be done. Unfortunately, many never make the first effort to make way towards better times. For me better times meant good-looking women and a nice bank account. This might sound like a plot to a low budget teen film, but for me it was only the truth. Many of the same people that laughed at my ideas then, we're then asking how they could get started themselves. Sure there was a little bit of enjoyment in the beginning knowing I had done something people (early co-workers) believed I could not do. Many of those same co-workers actually worked for me not so long afterwards, keeping books and searching talent. If I had believed anyone's criticism, I would not be anywhere near where I'm at today. Once my friends saw progress they were anxious to further help me with their ideas. Instead of hearing "cant be done", I was now hearing "what could be done". My friends enjoyed adult films just as much as I did, and they offered much help with ideas and work. So I say this. Since your reading this book, we share the same interest. For the past few years I have debated privately about writing this book. After all, I would be giving away my secrets to anyone who wished to enter this industry. Like I said earlier I have been involved in the adult industry for many years and as I have gotten older my life has taken different paths. These paths of course are good but a lot has changed since I first started making adult films. I have many other hobbies such as working with computers. I am currently working on business projects developing new software and I love every bit of it. I am also in the process of building a family. Eventhough I retired from making adult films because of these changes (especially the family part); I never once left the industry professionally in disappointment whatsoever. For every year I worked in the adult industry, I was very profitable both financially (thank goodness) and personally. Since I am working towards other passions, I decided to write this book after all. After thinking it over, I made the decision to pass on any help to anyone with the same interest. A large part was to help anyone who may be in same situation I was faced with many years ago. I never forget those hard days working at other jobs, hating every minute of it. I felt it was my duty to share my story and past experience.

Model Release Forms

The model release form is a piece of important document stating the actress gives you permission for you to sell the video she starred in. **It's a very important contract. It's very crucial that you have anyone starring in your video to sign it separately.** This should be done before any film is made with that particular actress/actor. This agreement is **very important**, and should not be taken lightly or disregarded. Without the model release, you basically invite yourself to be sued. When your tape does become a big success, the last thing you want is to pay large sums of the profits to the actress/actor. This can easily happen, all because they did not sign a model release, which legally lacks permission from them concerning the sale of the tape. What I recommend is having a local business attorney write up a simple contract/model release form. Believe me, you will be glad you did. I've heard many horror stories with this very subject. It has costed many x-film producers a lot of money for this simple mistake. **Do not let it happen to you.** After you have an attorney make up a simple model release, just take it and make some copies of the form (for later use) and everything is taken care of. **That form is your protection policy.** Along with other important documents (such as the actors/actresses 2 photocopied ID's), place everything in your file cabinet (preferably) for easy storage. As a filmmaker and businessperson, that file cabinet is your insurance policy in case you ever have to use it.

What should I do if the model doesn't want to sign the Release?

If the actress for whatever reason refuses to sign the release form, she just turned down the job. This rarely happens. For the most part, I've never had any problems getting an actress to sign the release form. If it does happen for any reason, she/he cannot be in the film. Period the end.

Special Note* If you have a married couple who would like to star together, have each sign a separate release form.

When you meet with women (who want to star), what do they often ask you?

When I have met women in the past they often have many questions for me to answer. Such questions, as how did you get started in this industry or how long have you been doing this kind of work? Since I've been in this business for over 12 years, I've got in the habit of telling them before they ask. Sometimes they ask me what my hobbies are. I inform them I love to workout (when I can), and working with computers. So when you have that meeting, expect to hear some questions aimed your way. Try to show as much confidence, but try not to act overconfident. An over confident attitude will make you come across as being a novice. If the woman doesn't have any words to say, encourage her to ask you some questions. It's a lot better to get everything out there on the table instead of dealing with it later on. Also, don't hesitate to ask her if she has any friends who might also be interested in adult film work. You never know, she could have three maybe four girlfriends who are drop dead gorgeous. This woman and her friends could be the entire cast of one of your films. Plus, not to mention, some of her girlfriends could have two or three friends as well. See where I'm going with this? Having a meeting with one woman could also produce 5 or 6 of her girlfriends for that project or any upcoming projects. Also, consider this scenario. From past experience, I've noticed and learned that when 1-woman stars in one of my films, usually her girlfriends will also want to star but for almost half the wage. So if actress A gets a wage of 200 dollars, her friend actress B will usually settle for only 100, sometimes even lower! You would be really surprised at how much money I have saved based on this referral process.

Remember, with every deal you close, ask her for referrals (anyone she knows 18+ who might be interested in starring).

After you have closed the deal with an actress, the only thing left is setting up a time to film the actual movie. Inform her of all details, such as location (ex. hotel), what you would like her to wear, and what sexual acts your looking to concentrate on the most. This should all be discussed before the date is set for filming. Always encourage questions. Get the facts then and there. If your planning to have someone else run the camera in which I recommend, let this be known to her ahead of time. If you can, introduce her to your cameraperson ahead of time as well. This will make it much easier when the time comes to start filming. It's really uncomfortable for anyone to have sex in front of someone they just met two minutes ago. If theres no time convenience for the actress to meet your cameraperson, tell the actress what kind of person they are, and what your cameraperson is like. When filming time comes, this inside information will help break the ice even further. It all comes down to saving time and making everything comfortable for your starlet. Get the comfort factor taken care of from the beginning, and the saving time part will take care of itself. As you can probably tell, I emphasize "saving time" a great deal. I firmly believe the old saying "time is money". **Very true indeed.**

Tell me more about Wardrobe?

To tell you the truth, have your actress's wear anything that turns you on. This does sound quite obvious, but I've had many people ask me this particular question. Me personally, I enjoy having the woman dress natural but revealing at the same time. I am a big fan of cut-off jean shorts ("daisy dukes"). Nothing drives me crazier than having a woman bend over in cut-offs with the edge of her cheeks glancing out. That's what I mean by natural but revealing. The human mind loves to wonder and dream. That's the minds defense mechanism for daily boredom. When someone sees too much to fast, their mind does not have enough time to process the fantasy. However, on the other hand when someone sees a beautiful woman with just a little bit revealing, then the possibilities to fantasize are endless. That's what I try to do in terms of wardrobe for my actresses. Another favorite revealing wardrobe I find excellent is bikinis. One of the best scenes in terms of this wardrobe is the "poolside shot". What I mean by the poolside shot, is having the woman's body in the pool with the water cutting below her breasts. This is a very revealing shot, and with the water adding sparkle makes it even better. Also, for pool shots, it always helps to have a tan actress. This will bring out a sexy glow. With most of the films I have shot, I have always preferred my actresses to have nice tans. Most of them usually used sunless tanning products to achieve a bronzed look. The reason I prefer tans on my actresses is because it covers any blemishes or redness that may appear. It gives the body a smooth sexy look. Quality all the way. I also prefer women with long hair. I have no idea why many women today simply cut their hair short. Very few women look good with short hair. The look of your actresses will determine how well your video sells. The reason I am mentioning these physical features with these qualities, is that they (movies with these physical qualities) have dramatically sold the most. Anyone can really go and find some women downtown and put together a cheap flick. However, believe it or not, very few take the time to pick quality starlets. Believe when I say, this time taking search will pay off greatly. Once the film is finished, you have a quality **product** (your product) to sell. When you market your product to distributors, you will be proud and the film will sell itself.

Have you Ever used the same Women in other videos?

Oh of course. I've made many friendships with many actresses from past work. They are some of the nicest people I have ever met. Before I got into this business I kinda thought many had troubled lives or drug problems (true in some cases unfortunately). However, the actresses that starred in my movies are some of the most well adjusted intelligent individuals you could ever meet. I have always enjoyed their company and openness. Their openness towards sex and there own desires is what truly helps me learn more. A producer or director did not teach me the experience I've had in filmmaking. I was trained by my own tastes and from most of the actresses I hired. I was always learning more and more with each film I produced. I've had instances during filming where my mind was just completely blocked out. For a producer/director that is the worst. Then the actress might suggest an idea that breaks the mental block. Sometimes that's how you learn. Sometimes instead of hiring an actress, you also get an consultant. Having a woman's opinion can be extremely valuable when making X-films. This is valuable since most women are taught how to get the man's attention. Sex appeal is also marketing appeal, both personal & financial. If something looks good, the attention will follow. Women love attention.

Produce a video with attractive women, and you will attract the attention of paying customers.

If you did so well producing and selling your own tapes why are you giving all your secrets away?

The simple reason is this. Currently, I am in the process of building a family and working towards other passions such as developing computer software. When I started producing adult films in the beginning, yes I did want to make a lot of money and yes I wanted to get laid all the time. But this was based on pleasure and not greed. I personnally welcome anyone to come into this business and make a name for themselves. Like I said, I'm also a fan. I want to go into the stores and see someone elses work. I want them to take me on a sexual journey. I want to see everything unfold in front of my eyes. Unfortunately, like I've said before, theres very few films that show the effort of turning someone fully on. Many will say, if theres so many of these films on the market then someone must be getting turned on? The truth is, some of these films do sell, but the problem is shelf life. A crappy film is gone before you can blink an eye. Next time your in an adult video store, take special notice of the films on the shelf that particular day. Then go back to that same exact store a month later and look at the selection. You will notice the films that were there last month are no longer there. Instead, they are replaced by similar movies which look no different. The movies that do remain, are the ones that sell/rent the most. That's the point I'm trying to make. With a quality film (with attractive women), the self life is much greater and your profits will be much greater.

For the most part, I use to visit adult video stores at least twice a week. Just like anyone else, when I walked into an adult video room, I started glancing. I usually started at one end and work my way through the entire selection. This is where the front cover of your movie box comes in.

The front cover. Probably the most important thing in the world for your video is the front cover of the box. I have seen excellent box covers portraying beautiful looking women, then when I got home and pushed "play" on the vcr, I wondered if they were the same starlets? That's what I call "a great marketing package for no package". You see a beautiful starlet on the box cover, then you get home and watch with disappointment. If I honestly thought about one of my customers watching one of my films and being disssappointed, it would bother me. I've never felt good about letting someone down, and that goes for anything. I like to shape my film box designs with the saying of "what you see is what you get". If you pick up one of my boxes to one of my films with a sexy starlet on the cover, she will look the same or if not better when you watch the film. My goal as the producer is to turn you on like no other film has, and for you to rent/buy my films over and over.

Film Content

With the sexual content of my films, sometimes adding kinky scenes will help enhance any picture. For the most part, my films relayed actual sex, oral, and threesomes. Kinky films dealing with dominatrix have been very popular so far, but these types of films are not making as much money as they use to. I have never really been a big fan of mixing pain with sexual pleasure. However, if these types of films turn you on, then there's a chance you could offer something these other dominatrix films lack. You might have that special ingredient people are looking for. For the foreign market, dominatrix films have continued to be especially popular throughout Europe and parts of Asia. The foreign adult video market is growing stronger and larger each day for American made films. Which is very good news for you. There is great earning potential to be made overseas. Many newcomers to the adult industry tend to overlook the foreign market. With current trends, neglecting this market would be a mistake. In the past, I have done just as well overseas than right here in the United States. Foreign countries also tend to treat sexual content much lighter than here in the U.S.

Video Cameras

If you don't already own a video camera, renting one instead would be the most cost effective. You can rent video cameras practically anywhere. The prices for rental usually range anywhere from $30-$75 per day. Some places will charge that same amount for two days or more. If your budget is limited at the moment, renting a video camera will save you much money and will do the job just as well. You really don't have to go out and spend hundreds or thousands of dollars on a camera. If you're planning to film out of town rent the camera there when you arrive. Avoid taking a rented camera with you on an out of town journey. This would be very expensive and it would be extemely risky to have a missing or damaged camera at the airport. Furthermore, with the type of video camera to rent, in terms of x-films, any type of camera will do just fine. The types of video cameras I used in the past were not anything super fancy. I enjoy **simplicity**. Most video cameras on the market today require you to read a 100 page manual with tons of complicated details. This can all be avoided with just a simple camera. It will save you much time and frustration. Call ahead to the local camera shops (Yellow Pages) and check prices, discounts, specials, any deposits, and once you find the best deal reserve it immediately. Remember to ask for any add-ons, such as a fixated adjustable light. This is the light that attaches to the top of the camera. When filming in rooms with level lighting (lamps), your picture will have dark shadows. The reason for this, is because with level lighting the light directly reflects with the camera lens. The simple solution to this problem is adding an attachable light to the tip of your camera. Having this light will eliminate any shadows on your finished film. If the room your shooting in has ceiling lights, this should not produce any shadows from appearing in your film (since the light source is shining down instead of shining level).

However, even if you have ceiling lights, I still recommend using the attachable light. In person the room will seem bright enough, but from the video standpoint it will be a few shades darker. Most camera stores that offer video camera rentals will usually provide the attachable lights with the rental. Some may add a small charge or fee for the light. The only thing I can say is, make sure you have that light before you start filming.

Note* Again, I highly recommend having and using the attachable light with any room environment. "Better safe than sorry"!

The camera tripod. This is another extra piece of equipment I strongly recommend having before your shooting begins. Some camera shops will include the tri-pod with the camera rental. Some shops may charge a small fee. Having a tripod will greatly reduce camera shaking. Films with saturated shaking will produce a dizzy effect on your audience, in all the wrong ways.

When you decide to do business with a camera shop, reserve **ALL** pieces of equipment. Never assume after having the camera reserved, that the other pieces, such as the attachable light will be available. **Make sure to reserve all pieces (light attachment, tripod, and of course the camera itself).**

What about video Editing?

Most of today's camcorders have sophisticated editing capabilities. However, If you're interested in some good photo editing software, you can try the different versions of Pinnicle or In-Sync. The prices for different software packages will vary.

37

Since your just starting out, I would recommend starting with the least expensive package. Then from there, once your business begins to really grow, you can always upgrade if you ever need any extras.

You can reach Pinnicle's website at www.pinnaclesys.com. And In-Sync can be reach at www.in-sync.com.

Again the majority of your expense will come from paying the actresses to star. However, with Spring break, you could end up with two films or more for under $200. As crazy as it sounds, it can easily be done. When hiring a topless dancer, you could be paying between $175 to $200. However, I have been really surprised with many (attractive) topless dancers willing to star for under $100. It just all depends on the woman and the circumstances.

Have you ever had Any problems with women backing out or changing their minds?

Yes. On some occasions there have been times where an actress backed out at the last possible minute. When making adult films, you can unfortunately expect this to happen at times. I've had scenarios where the woman was ready and full willing to do the scene. Then at the drop of a hat, claimed she wasn't interested anymore and had changed her mind. All I can say is, this is very frustrating considering the wasted time and money (on hotel rooms etc).

Important Tip * Always remember to pay your actresses/actors after their work is completed. If you pay them before the work is done, they may not want to give the money back to you. This has happened before believe it or not. An actress was paid up front, backed out, then had the nerve to ask "why should I give the money back to you?". Again, very frustrating if you make the mistake of paying anyone before the scene is completed. This occurrence can be completely avoided if you follow the above rule.

Another fairly common problem with some starlets is not following direction during filming. Before I film anyone, I always ask them if there's anything they won't do or is there anything that makes them uncomfortable? Sometimes you can expect a young woman to be fully open for doing certain acts. Then when filming begins, she'll begin to say how she can't do this or that. During those times it's real easy to show your anger, but as a professional you have to work around any problems that arise. This by any means isn't always simple.

How long does it usually take to shoot one film?

Your first adult film depending on many circumstances could take you anywhere from 1 week to two months to make. I would say no more than two or three months to shoot a really decent adult feature. The films I have produced in the past have taken me one to four weeks on average to make. This time range has a lot to do with finding the right talent for my film needs. I have passed up on many young women. I was very picky when it came to choosing talent. If I'm going to pay someone, then that someone has to be right from the very beginning. This has to do with my own personal tastes and my audience's taste. Furthermore, when I took a trip to Vegas or Springbreak, I could have one or two films made less than a week easy. Plus, not to mention at a very low cost. All I can say is, take special time when putting your film together. This is especially true if it's your first film. Remember, with special time and work, this film could bring you major profits for many years to come. Having a strong film product to show for will also make your marketing campaign much easier. Since your money and time is being invested, it's worth to take your time and enjoy yourself along the way.

How much time should you break in between from filming your first and second movies?

After you have finished filming your first film, concentrate on marketing that product before filming your second film. When you start out marketing your first film, you will come into contact with many stores & distributors (discussed later). After you have established some sales with such clients, you will then have an established business relationship with them. Chances are in your favor, that if someone (stores&distributors) purchases your first video then they will buy from you again and again, many times over.

If your first film is carelessly made, this will automatically create a bad impression with the distributors and video stores. Like I said, the competition of bad skin flicks come and go. The good ones stay around and make handsome profits year after year. When distributors/video stores see a sample of your product and what it offers, they will most likely be interested. As long as their customers are buying/renting, they will have no problem ordering more copies and different videos from you. When this happens, watch your bank balance grow and grow. That's how the adult industry has produced many multi- millionaires. Take it from me, this industry if done wisely will **treat you right**.

What about Marketing?

Marketing your films can be fun, but it can also represent the most work. When you start marketing your film product in the beginning, you will find yourself on the phone quite often. After you close your first deal with a distributor/video store, you will be hooked. When you earn your first profits from the work you put in, the feeling is very fulfilling. All it takes is a little patience and some organization, and you are already halfway there. Because as long as man and woman are walking the earth, there will always be a large demand for sex related products, with millions of people willing to pay money for it. **Always will.** In fact, with the millions of people online these days, did you know the #1 searched keyword in every major search engine is the word "sex"? Not to mention, the next nine top keywords are also related to sex! Keywords such as naked and breasts, make up the top 10. This isn't a U.S. statistic, **it's a global one!** It really shows where people's minds are.

What time of day are the Films usually shot?

The time of day you shoot your film really doesn't matter. All you have to do is pick a time that's convenient for you, the cameraperson, and actress.

What about outdoor scenes?

Early in my career almost all of my films were shot in inside/room sequence. This is where the woman comes in, moves to the bed, then so on. After a couple years of starting, I decided to do some outdoor scenes, which I thought would be fun to do. I love making poolside scenes. They are my favorite types of outdoor scenes to shoot. I think every man sometime in his life, has seen a perfectly gorgeous woman lying out in the sun, and further wishing he could have sex with her right then and there. Beach scenes offer the same scenerio. We have all been to the beach and seen a woman we wanted to have sex with. I love adult films centered on showing reality with a mix of erotic possibilities. I want to place the viewer in a familiar place they have been before, but with a much better outcome. When you sell an adult video, you are not presenting someone just a tape with sex on it; instead you are sharing a dream. You are selling them an escape from daily reality. Again, this is only from a well crafted film. A well-crafted film is actually less stressful to make. The reason for this? Because you simply construct something you would buy/rent yourself in a store. If your fantasy is to have two women in a pool with you, then there's a very strong chance millions of men also share that fantasy. That could be your first movie. True, you see two women with one guy on many box covers, but very few have "attractive" natural women. Your audience wants to see you with women that would <u>never</u> seem the type to be in adult films.

This again does have a lot to do with personal taste. Again, if you like brunettes with long hair, chances are millions of men do to (including me).

How can you tell if a particular Woman is right for one of your Films?

Most of the women for obvious reasons will be quite shy when you first meet them face to face. That's why it's important to just have fun with good conversation. You'll notice later on in the conversation how much their true personality will start to come out. If the woman seems hesitant throughout the entire meeting, then chances are she might back out during filming.

On the other side of the coin, you have women who talk a great game then back out. In the past, I have had meetings with very confident sexual women. Then have that same type of woman get shy once the camera started to film. However, it is normal to expect some level of shyness from these women; in essence it's part of the turn-on. Since it shows naturalness. So you can expect most actresses to be nervous, but some will require some extra time to relax. Giving your actresses patience will in the long run make your filming experience go smoother.

When you shot your first film, how long did it take to get over your own Nerves?

For me, I had to go through the same bit of nervousness. After all, this is adult video. I stayed relatively nervous until seven months after my first film. This will gradually fade away as you make more films. It will definitely boost the confidence level much further. Thinking and actual doing, are entirely two different points. You might start out with thoughts like "I'm not sure if I can do this" to " there's nothing to it". Before I began shooting, I told my actresses I could relate to them in terms of nervousness. I openly informed them, that I have been where they are. Once you tell someone you can relate, for some reason this helps them to relax. People sometimes, just want to be understood. **Showing an understanding will strengthen the comfort zone, with the women you work with.**

Did you personally star in all of your movies?

From the very beginning I mostly starred/acted in my movies. Afterwards, I wanted to be behind the camera, to get the exact shots I wanted. I really like to be in control of filming. If I am starring in one of my films, I am often worried about how certain shots will come out. That's why I love to be behind the camera. Because I know that this film is going to be a finished product and that it will have to be marketed. If I'm doing the filming, I have no one to blame but myself.

With choosing actors to star, at one time, I had my bestfriend do the scenes. Marty still remains a close friend, and he always took his work seriously. A lot of guys who have starred in adult films are often to busy showing off. The funny thing is, people really don't want to see them, they want to see the starlet. Marty was a total pro. He was very patient and calm. A lot of actors tend to rush the scene. It's only natural for males to rush when in the presence of a gorgeous female. If you do not wish to star in your own films, find someone who will take it professionally just as you would. If I had picked some of my other friends, they might constantly laugh and joke throughout the entire shoot. Remember, you will have many nervous women in your presence. The last thing you want is a bunch of guys making crude jokes. My other friends are great people, but I was against having them there while filming. In fact when you set out to put a film together, do not take more than two people with you. I would actually recommend only you and someone to run the camera. That would be it besides the actress/actresses. Time is money. This will be a finished product that people will pay for. If you have a bunch of guys hanging around, your filming will be a complete disaster. One time I did have a couple friends come to the set, with the actress's approval of course, and the whole day fell apart. I had some great scenes on film but with them talking in the background. I was so angry, but at myself. **A hard lesson learned**. Remember, as fun as making adult films sounds, it is after all a business. The footage you shoot for your film will be paid for by **your** money and time. Just you and someone to run the camera should be present, to work with the actress/actresses. If after filming you decide to have a party, invite your friends then.

How do some women feel about getting involved with adult films?

Most of the actresses after finishing a film seemed really surprised they didn't have feelings of guilt. I have always made certain, that each actress had sincere knowledge of what they were getting involved with. I was not in business to create guilt but pleasure. Some X-producers unfortunately look at their models as pieces of meat. I am 100% against looking at another individual as being disposable. If you respect others, they will respect you in return. I have always lived by that saying.

How did your own parents feel about you being involved with adult films?

For me, my parents were very supportive. They know I am a good person with good morals. At first, they were not to thrilled with the fact I was involved with adult filmmaking. Afterwards, they didn't see it as being harmful. They noticed I practiced good morals and ethics within my work. However, some politicians might disagree with the morals part.

How did you market the films you made to Video Stores?

When the time comes to start marketing your film, there are many different areas to consider. You could market your product directly to the public or sell your films to video stores. I think one of the easiest ways to make your profits quickly is to sell them directly to the video stores. This will in part cut your advertising costs almost completely. The only cost may be the telephone call. With the adult film business all it takes is a decent product, mail, and a telephone.

The number of video stores that carry adult films will always continue to grow rapidly in numbers. With some stores, adult films tend to account for almost 60% of the stores profits. In some cases that figure is actually much greater. With that figure in mind, you can be certain there is a large demand for adult films. Remember, all together this industry is a multi-billion dollar industry. This number continues to grow incredibly each year. Again the market will always be there. Your goal is to get a nice piece from this industry. Out of billion +dollars generated, making 150 to 400 thousand dollars a year is very attainable, and this is for the first few years! If you run your business right, this figure is not as difficult as you might think. Once you have your film packaged (discussed later) and copyrighted, you are ready to move forward. Before you make any calls, take out a sheet of paper and write down every quality of your film that you can. Such qualities could be very attractive women (very important), the number of scenes, and so on. After you have written down these qualities, all you need now is a list of video store telephone numbers. Obtaining these telephone numbers is very simple. You could go to your local library and look at the business directory, which covers, nationwide and international. Most libraries carry a business directory located in the <u>reference section</u>. I highly recommend using it. It can be a major time saver, when searching for potential video stores to sell to.

Once you have a selected list of video store telephone numbers, the only thing left to do is call. When you call some stores, you might have to get another phone number from them. That number will most likely be the headquarters, for that particular video chain. Once in contact, ask how you can reach that company's buyer. Once they put you through to the buyer, pitch your film slowly and clearly. In the past, whenever I pitched my video sales message to fast, the buyer usually never took me serious. It made me come across as being amateur. Once I began to relax, my sales message to the stores came without much effort.

What do stores request during telephone calls made to them?

When you contact video stores, some will request a sample of your tape. Again, before you send out any tape, make sure you have it copyrighted or pending copyright. When you send your film, include a personal letter, detailing whom you talked with from their store. Also, mention the qualities of your film again (brief), and have your business logo at the top of your personal letter. At the bottom of your typed letter, add your signature with blue ink (makes it more personal, since it shows you didn't photo copy your signature).

Place your film (tape) in a protective sleeve, label it, and send it to its proper destination. With postage, it really shouldn't cost you more than four or five dollars to send it. Once you start sending more mailings, you should qualify for a **"bulk mailing permit"** at your local post office. When that time comes, ask your local post office for details.

How many mailings should one start out with?

When you start your search for video stores to call, start out by contacting anywhere from 5 to 10 right at first. Most stores will usually be acceptable to view your sample. After you contact 5 to 10, stay with them and make some follow-up calls to those same original stores. After some time has passed, begin with another 5 to 10 video stores to contact. Make sure you have a log (book) to keep track of all business calls and any samples that have been sent out. Having well-organized records is crucial. Keep track of everything from the very beginning. Write down the person's name you talked with, and the date/time of day you talked with them. Having these records will be critical for making follow-up calls, and will show you which stores requested a sample tape. Having organized records will make your follow-up phone calls much easier. Follow-ups are essential for your business growth. When you make a follow-up phone call, it shows confidence in your product. Believe it or not, many producers are actually embarrassed about their work. With complete confidence in your work, you will never have to worry about this.

How long is the shelf life for an Adult film?

A well-made film with very attractive women could have the shelf life of many years. There are films that were made in the mid-80's that remain on the shelf even to this day. This is especially true in foreign markets. A film with unattractive women will not be on the store shelf long. They usually disappear as fast as they come in.

Have you Ever had some of your films not do so well in terms of selling?

In the past, I've had some films do extremely well in terms of sales. I have had some do fairly decent, and I've had some not do so well. I quickly realized how important packaging your films was. Having the best possible poses (actresses posing) on the front of your film box cover is crucial to its success. The idea when packaging your box cover, is to not show too much. This is especially true for the front cover of your box. The back of the box can be a little more revealing. Also, your **film** boxes cannot show any sexual penetration or open genitals due to new laws. Next time you view an X-rated movie box, notice how the genitals are clouded out. Always remember to cloud out any areas that show open genitals (Duplicators can do this for you...discussed later). I personally recommend not revealing too much on your movie box cover. A simple picture of one of your starlets posing on a bed will do just fine. With your pictures, make sure to have your starlets show such features like her face, legs and butt. Also, for the back of your film box, another great tip would be to have your pictures printed upside down. This will make any hopeful paying customer look twice. Again, make your box covers sexy but not to revealing. True, you want your box cover to turn people on, but by making it less revealing, it will accomplish this. I particularly love seeing women in tight bikinis on front box covers. I almost always pick up this type of film box when browsing through a selection. Cute natural women posing on beds is a sure attention getter, and these movies seem to be rented out more often than others. Another great picture shot to put on your front box cover is to have two women posing together on a bed. Simply have the two women look ahead and smile while sitting next to one another. This will gain the curiosity of potential customers to buy/rent your film. If they see to much action on your box, then the curiosity will be gone. Without this curiosity, expect your sales to be very low. I can't understand why some adult film producers choose to over do the content on their film box covers. It really does amaze me. I've come to the conclusion, that maybe they do not care. Personally, I think they are crazy, since they could gain much better profits from their films.

How easy is it to find women who are willing to do a scene with another woman?

Most women, who are willing to star in adult films, are usually willing to do a sex scene with another woman. When I was in the beginnings of starting out, I was often embarrassed to ask another woman if she would be willing to do a girl/girl scene. I was really surprised how many seemed ok to do this type of scene work. Furthermore, it is of most importance to have at least one girl/girl scene in your movie. This type of scene will always be in demand. It's literally a bare essential to include a girl/girl scene. Always remember to place the girl/girl segment in the middle of your films. Never start your film with the girl/girl segment right away. Even if you are a big fan of lesbianism, it's so much better to have the scenes work into the lesbian scene. Now if you decide to have a complete lesbian film, then obviously you don't have to worry about segment placing by this category.

Are group sex films big sellers in today's market?

Movies that solely depict group sex, have started to really blossom in terms of profits. These types of films have begun to take over shelves at many adult stores. I have produced a couple of these films, and for the most part they were quite fun to make. I particularly loved to produce scenes with threesomes. Threesomes are my favorite, in terms of group sex. For a producer, they are a lot easier to make compared to having 10 people all at once. When there are 10 or more people involved in a sex scene, it does in my opinion take away some excitement (this of course depends on the person). The reason I express that opinion is because the viewer's mind has to concentrate on many things all at once. Which makes it difficult to imagine oneself in the fantasy. If a scene is completely unrealistic, then it will be very difficult for the viewer to place themselves inside that world created on film. Now don't get me wrong, there are many great 10+ person scenes out there, but they are very few and far between.

Group sex films are earning decent profits, but the shelf life of these films still remains very short.

How did you keep in contact with some of the girls you have worked with in the past?

Try to stay in touch with past talent. Always keep their phone number and an email address (if they have one) on their Identification/Model release form (this should be there regardless). If you ever run into a shortage for finding talent, your only a phonecall away from your past talent. I've had some cases where I had to do just that. I had one film in particular, which lacked one starlet (who originally backed out). I picked up the phone and in five minutes I had a fill in. It's especially easier to work with girls you have already had experience with. They basically know what to expect and they already feel comfortable filming around you. Since the two of you already know one another, filming can take place almost immediately after her arrival.

As time passes, you can expect this list of past talent to grow very quickly.

How many segments should one have in a film?

Most adult films have at least three segments. This is the minimum norm. Most of my films contained three to four segments. I am a firm believer in giving my audience a good show with great talent. With three to four segments, I hope to get my fellow viewer off in the first. If for some reason I am unable to do this, the next two or three surely will.

Always have your segments set up so they are carried out completely before moving on to the next. I have viewed a number of films where they take you from one story to the next, then back again. Nothing could be more annoying to the viewers. I often call this style of segment placing" the soap opera effect". Drives me nuts. Especially when it's a great film. Nothing is more disappointing than to watch a movie that brings the fantasy into full effect, then all of a sudden your watching something else. I often compare it to blowing a game with a 7-point lead in the ninth inning. Since you already have someone worked up in the fantasy, it's only necessary to finish the job before moving on to the next sequence. I think this makes perfect sense. Again, what makes a great film is the tease effect. Your viewers are begging to be teased. **Begging for it.**

When you sold your videos by phone to video stores what could you Expect?

When you begin making calls to video stores to make sales, you could expect many things. Often enough, whenever one sounds not interested, tease them with an offer to ship a sample. Most places will almost always accept a sample. **With your samples do not send the entire film with all three or more segments.** The reason I say this is because they could take your sample and place it on their shelves. If they do this, which is totally wrong, they are making money off a free tape (plus disregarding your copyright, which gives you an easy lawsuit).

What you do is place about ten minutes of your best material on the sample tape. With your sample, it's perfectly fine to show a few minutes from different segments. **Remember, this is a sample not a full feature.** The samples entire purpose is to give any video store/distributor an idea of what your film offers. Another tip would be to send the sample in a clear sleeve. **Do not send the final promotional box to them.** Someone could take your box and your footage, combine it with other sources and use your box to market it. This however is illegal for anyone to do, considering and hoping you have everything copyrighted before conducting business. With a small sample of footage and clear sleeve, include a picture of your box cover (front, back) instead of the actual box. The reason for sending pictures of your film box is to give the video store an idea of what their customers will see on first impression.

Sending pictures is safer than sending the <u>actual</u> cover.

When should you Expect a video store/distributor to return a call or give you an answer concerning your sample tape?

After you have mailed your sample to a video store/distributor, wait no more than a week to follow-up. If no store/distributor has returned with a phone call, call them no later than one week. When you place your follow-up phone call, ask to speak to the same person you talked to before. Asked them if they received your film,

54

and ask them for there opinion concerning your film. If they have not yet viewed your sample film, ask when they might be able to view it. Again, tell them your sample is only 10 to 15 minutes long (these are busy people). Inform them that your films have received great reviews from other stores. After two or three days, do not hesitate to call them again, if they have not contacted you after the first follow up phone call. Persistence is the key. Simply giving up on a certain store could cost you plenty of money in the years to come. Video store buyers stay busy constantly. After making several phone calls, they will remember you. That's what you want. Keep in mind, that these same stores will be interested in buying from you over and over again. Once you establish a working relationship, it almost like owns stock. For years to come, you could be earning a fortune for the films you made during the previous years. Remember to keep accurate records with all names of video store buyers in a safe place. Once you start conducting business with a large number of stores, it will be extremely easy to lose track of who you talked with on any given occasion. Keep good records. Stay organized with every business contact and what they have ordered from you in the past. This will come in handy when your films start rolling into video stores. If you need to go back and find something, your records will be there to back everything up for you. **Remember to keep your actress/model files separate from your video store business files.** If you have a file cabinet, keep these two types of file categories in separate drawers.

Is it Easier to sell directly to distributors than Video stores?

Distributors will make things a lot easier for you in terms of moving large volumes of tapes quickly. With video stores, there are so many different outlets. When you sell to a distributor, they

will buy certain quantities from you, then sell your films to the video stores themselves. Distributors are the "middle-men". They will save you much time in terms of contacting video stores compared to doing it on your own. However, when your just starting out, I think it would be better to sell directly to the video stores yourself. Since video stores greatly outnumber distributors, it will give you the opportunity to earn money a lot quicker. When you sell directly to the video stores you will earn a higher profit for each tape, than if you were to sell to a distributor. When the demand for your films has dramatically increased, then it's easier to sell directly to the distributor. This is mainly out of the time consideration you will be saving yourself. There is one major distributor that represents a major force in the adult industry. The name of this distributor is **"General Video of America"** (G.V.A.). The very famous V.C.A. video production company uses G.V.A. for distributing their films. G.V.A. is located in Canoga Park, CA (outside of Los Angeles). Their telephone number is (818) 407-9990. If you would like to write to them there address is:
General Video of America Inc
6617 Independence Avenue, Canoga Park, CA 91303.

Special Note* <u>You have nothing to lose.</u> **Once your film is finished and <u>copyrighted</u>, contact the above distributor (G.V.A.). With adult film distribution, they are the largest. And I mean large.** <u>You have nothing to lose.</u> **Call them, locate their buyer, and offer a 10 to 15 minute sample of your movie. If they want the entire feature, this is the only case where it's ok. This company is highly respected and well established. If they decline your offer, just keep calling, and mail your film anyway (directed to the buyer). If this one company buys from you right away, you will have a smile on your face for a very long time. To give you an idea on what I'm talking about, picture every video store with an adult video room and every adult novelty store,,,,GVA has supplied practically each one. That's a lot of stores my friend. Think about it. Multiply just a**

tiny fraction of the number of stores, by the cost of your movie. *I'll see you on the beach.*

Another great distributor, which deals specifically with adult video mail order, is **"Excalibur Films"**. They claim to be one of the largest adult mail order distributors in the world. Their address and telephone number is below:

Excalibur Films (714) 773-5855
3621West Commonwealth Ave.
Fullerton, CA 92833

Some Important Questions To Ask Distributors.

-What's the distributor's overall eagerness towards your film/films?

-How does the distributor demonstrate its enthusiasm, to give your films an extra thrust?

-Are the distributors personnel able to pay close attention to your films?

-Is the distributor responsive in developing a close relationship with you, the producer?

-How well known is the distributor? How much experience does this distributor have with marketing and promoting adult films?

-Can this distributor give further guidance or extra advice for your films marketing capability?

-What are the distributors catalogs, brochures, and other printed materials like in terms of feature, organization and arrangement? How many are issued? And how often are they issued?

-Can this distributor acquire a marketing plan with precise projections?

-Can this distributor furnish breakdowns "percentages" of users?

-What warranties does the distributor honor? In conjunction with the number of video stores your films will be distributed or sent to?

-How well known is this distributor with the competition?

-Does this distributor have methods for marketing adult films based on regional areas?

-Does this distributor have any extra methods for moving your film into video store outlets?

-What's the bulk of this distributor's mailing index? Is direct mail effectively put to use?

-How is this distributors advertising budget concluded?

-Does this distributor use distinct companies for foreign and domestic circulation?

-How capable is the distributor computer/record keeping procedure in how it indicates sales, rentals, and consumer obligations?

-How does the distributor deal with returns?

-What rights do you, the filmmaker hold (ex. international distribution)?

-Does this company go into alliance with other companies for certain regions?

-Who pays for varied advertising costs?

-What **ratio** of gross sales and/or earnings is yielded to you the producer? <~~~~ **that's a big one** ~~~~

-How are gross receipts determined and from what sources?

-How often are royalties collected to **you** the producer?

-How does the company track revenue origins?

-If representatives or subdistributors are used, how much of that sales gross goes to the innovator?

-How is the pricing of your films determined?

-Can you the producer inspect the distributor's financial register?

*I know it's a lot to take in, but these questions are narrowed by being the most important.

Have you Ever had any problems with any particular stores or distributors?

Some stores no matter how hard you try, will not be interested in carrying your product (movie). This can be expected with any type of product no matter what it may be. Some video stores refuse to carry adult oriented movies. Most however, in most parts of the country do. Certain states like Florida and North Carolina have been known to have strict laws concerning X- rated films being carried in retail video stores. For every store not interested in viewing your sample, you could expect three or four that will. Most stores that carry adult oriented films know how profitable they are, and what they are capable of. After you have made at least two follow up phonecalls to any particular store, if they are not interested at that point forget about them. **This however depends on the size of their company or their overall chain...always stay persistent with the <u>big stores</u>. To find out how big they are, simply ask when you call. Ask each video store you contact how many stores they have? How long have they been in business? And most important, do they carry adult films in any of their stores?**
If a small tiny video store turns down your offer, don't feel bad. Move on, and forget it.

I compare it to fishing. Who in the world is going to <u>care</u> if a small fish refuses to take your bait???

You are out to catch the big ones. If the big one falls off your hook, re-bait and cast over and over again. <u>It's that simple.</u>

The wealthiest people in the world are the ones who <u>keep</u> casting. The rest pack up and go home.

Getting back....
The point is to keep contacting as many stores as you can. Many will be interested or curious to what you offer. Especially with a teaser of a sample clip. You will find many stores unable to turn down this offer. The name of the game is to make your offer

sweeter and sweeter. If you are unable to close a deal no matter what, bring your price down a little at a time. To make some profit, is a whole lot better than not making any. Plus, I will say it again; your gains will not only be financial, but also personal with the creation of a new business relationship. If any store can be sold to, based on bringing your price down a dollar per tape, by all means sell them the films. Establishing that business relationship is where the huge payoff resides. Plus, who says you can't raise the price a year later?

How long could Business Relationships last when you make them?

When you establish a working business relationship, you could expect them to last forever. Once you establish yourself with any particular store, the rest is cake. It's all about building trust with one another. Once you have your winning film in their stores, they will want more products from you. Within weeks of finishing your first film, you can start establishing positive business relationships with any video store in the country. A whole lot can be done by ways of mail and telephone. Most sales people take these 2 powerful tools for granted, or abuse them unconditionally. This is quite simple and may sound odd, but clear you mind right now and think about it for just 2 or 3 seconds. Right this very second, you have the power at your very fingertips to contact practically any business on the entire globe! You also have the complete power, to send a letter that you wrote, practically anywhere on the world's surface. With a total world population of 6 billion, there is no distance your message can't reach. And by all means, those tools are not the only ones. They simply scratch the surface. For fun, answer this question. Out of the 6 billion people on earth, how many were created without the gift of sex? Or better yet, how many would love to see that gift expressed in your movie? Thank you. Moving on....

Once your first film is made, you could make other films to follow behind it in the form of volume numbers. I have seen up to 90 films produced by the same individual in the same store. Most are multi-millionaires. By all means they aren't the only ones.

How many films should one make in a year?

The number of films you make in a year is entirely up to you and your budget. To really notice how your first film sells, it could take at least six months to really know. **However, I've had some cases where one of my films did not sell at all in the first six months. Then all of a sudden, that very same film took off and ended up being the most profitable film for years to come.** Sometimes things happen unexpectantly for better or worse. As long as you have confidence and pride in your work, you will never go wrong. With pride in your work, your enthusiasm will shine even brighter, especially when you start promoting. Pretending to have confidence in your work is very difficult to fake. That's why it is absolutely crucial to take your time making your film. Believe me, the patience and extra effort will pay off. When you make calls to video stores to sell your product, they will automatically sense the pride and confidence in your voice. If for any reason you sound uncertain to them, they will not be interested in seeing your work. Remember, these stores are out to make a profit also. They want films people will rent or buy. It's that simple. Once a company or individual rents or buys from you, they will then have more faith in you and your company. You have to convince stores or distributors, that you are willing to work faithfully to help both parties make handsome profits. Two of the biggest mistakes a newcomer makes, is giving up to quickly and not having 100% confidence in there work. Many newcomers wish to make a fast dollar without any effort. Again, you have to convince any company you wish to do business with, that you are interested in making profits with them, together. To work as a team. These stores will pay wholesale prices for your tapes, usually anywhere from $9.00 to $24.00 per tape. This is just a sample figure; it changes all the time company to company. You will have different price arrangements set with each store. **Never** disclose any price arrangements you have with other stores. This **will** hurt you in the end. Always keep prices confidential with each store or distributor, you do business with. You may sell the same tape with a ten-dollar price difference to another store. Some of this has to do with the number of tapes any store is willing to purchase from you. It's fairly known that, the more tapes you sell to any particular store, the higher the price break. This is essentially true. However, always start high when negotiating price. You want to give yourself plenty of room to bring your price down. Also, you want to start high so the other party (store) may settle close to the high price that you offered. Which means more profit for you. If you start to low, then you endanger yourself from making little or any profit. Keep the negotiating price as high as you can. You will be surprised at how often a buyer of a company, is quick and ready to settle. With this in mind, you could even try to set the negotiating price even higher with the next store you negotiate with. Always find limits to how high your price can go. Some stores will settle at a very high wholesale price. With the larger video chains, you will notice how quickly they can talk you down. This is fine, since these large chains have hundreds (if not thousands) of stores. Once you add up all the stores and the number of tapes you sell to fill each of them, then you can see how much money you can make. Better yet, some of these giant video chains are always building more stores and making existing stores bigger. With many private owned video stores, you will probably be able to sell at a higher profit. The only thing is, they may have only one or two stores. With the larger video chains, one phone call could determine you supplying hundreds or thousands of stores. Eventhough the profit rate per tape might be lower, the number of stores will make up the difference **many** times over. The key is getting the giant chain stores to stock your films. Some private establishments go out of business quite regularly. When you go to call any particular private store, you may find them no longer existing. With the chain stores you have a much better chance at keeping a long lasting relationship. Many local libraries have a "business directory" (located in the **reference section**), which lists any kind of major business you could think of in North America & internationally. This directory is your key to finding many businesses that might be interested in working with you. This directory is a very thick book and often enough most libraries will not let you take it home.

However, next time you're in the library, take a few minutes to look through this book. Take a sheet of paper and write some of the addresses & telephone numbers from some of the major video chains. The "Business Directory" will list secret facts for each business, such as company size, revenue generated, and so on. That's how you identify the big stores from the little ones. If you wish, ask the librarian for information on buying this directory from its source. This directory usually sells anywhere from $75 to $125 dollars. The librarian should have the address for the source. I must say how valuable this business directory has been for me. The information in it is truly priceless.

Since there are so many video stores throughout the country and world, your options and choices are practically **endless**. If even just a <u>fraction</u> of those stores, were to stock a few of your films, this could place you in a nice starting position financially. With a quality film in your possession, the odds are dramatically in your favor. The trick is to make the odds work for you. By taking action and believing, the rest is history. Always expect some setbacks.

They will happen. In the past I have been turned down many times. However, the day I made my first deal, I knew I could do it. **That's all it took.**

What about procrastination?

When you are in the process of starting out, you might have tendencies to procrastinate. All I can say is to take each day, step by step. Tomorrow will come whether you want it to or not. Try to keep everything **simple**. Take care of things that are most important during that specific time. After you have a finished product, and have made your first sales the rest will flow. People in general are only convinced after they see some form of result. That's the problem I think with trying anything new. To start fresh with no results, is perceived as very difficult or unrealistic. There is no magic wand that strikes someone; success with anything is built. What is done today will reflect tomorrow. Getting your first film made now will enable you to sell it tomorrow. When you sell your tapes, the only thing left is to deposit your checks. Then make more films. That's how money is made in this and any other business.

Making Mistakes

I have made many mistakes throughout my career. Mistakes are fine. Just remember them, so you don't repeat them. Or should I say cut down on them.

The biggest mistake you could possibly make is taking anything to harshly on yourself. That would be the biggest mistake. Anytime I have ever taken something to harshly; not one time did it make anything better. I solved nothing. Now of course, when you invest money and time into a project, and when something turns out wrong it's normal to be upset. Just remember, this happens to everyone who has ever made any type of film. At least with adult movies more is forgiven along the lines of camera angles. Many of your buyers will be forgiving. After all, this isn't going to be a film to win "Best Picture" at the Academy Awards. But, who knows, with the world changing so much, it wouldn't surprise me. It might win at the Adult Video Awards in Las Vegas though. You never know.

How much money does adult videos account for in sales with video store outlets?

The video stores that carry adult films and newly released mainstream films have been known to make the most profits. Such large video chains like "20 20 video" based in Los Angeles are just an example. Stores that offer adult films are extremely profitable outlets. In many cases, adult films represent anywhere from 35%-60% of total monthly revenue generated by these stores. That is serious market potential. These figures are not going down but are going up. Very fast. The end is nowhere near for the adult film. Adult films will continue to draw higher profits in the continuing years. It's the one industry that doesn't require a lot of money to produce. The audience and need for this audience will always exist. Like I was saying earlier, out of the millions of people online, the number one searched keyword is sex. **Again, that's a global statistic.**

How many store chains could one Expect to have Established business ties with?

Within your first year you could have established anywhere from 50 to 400+ stores. As you can already see, your first year could start by being very profitable. Within your very first week of marketing to stores, you could establish a working relationship with up to 10 or more stores. This number is just an example; there have been upstarts who have only produced 3 in the first week. However, these 3 stores could also be major video chains. Each chain representing anywhere from 45 to 1000 stores each. With this in mind, three isn't such a small number. As long as you have something to sell, the rest is just picking up the phone and negotiating. For me in the beginning that was a whole lot easier than doing landscaping. I would much rather pick up the phone and sell something I help created.

Throughout, one of the biggest lessons I learned was that selling a product is much better than selling a service. Now, as with any business you have to offer some kind of service, but what I'm getting at is the service one determinably pays you for. When someone gets paid for painting houses, they make their money with that service. When you begin to sell your product (films), the strain of labor will be no where near that of offering a service.

Since your tapes will be sold by ways of store, distributors, or directly to the public, customer service will not be as demanding for you.

When you sell directly to video stores or distributors, they will tell you if they they are interested in your film. If they purchase your film, since they thought it was good enough, usually will not complain if it did not sell.

Tell me more about Bulk sales?

Practically all of the chain stores (video stores & distributors) will purchase films in bulk from you. When a store buys bulk, they expect a nice discount. It just all depends on the store and their negotiating policies. Like I said earlier, I always start high with my price when negotiating. If the store is part of a major chain, I will further push the idea of getting my films sold to them in larger bulk quantities. There is so much opportunity with large chain outlets. Closing a deal with just one large chain video store could mean the difference between making up to $70 thousand extra dollars a year. That figure represents just one or two films. With a volume series ranging up to 50 films, $70 thousand is small. With large video chains you want to do everything possible to get their business. By all means never hesitant to give them a great deal. The average adult film to buy retails for $30. At wholesale the tape could sell for $10-$23. If a certain store buys 25 of my films, I will usually sell my film to them for $15 each. This comes to $375 profit minus the cost of the actual videocassette. If another video store offers to purchase 400 of my films, I will usually sell my film for $10 each. Let's do the math. That deal from one film would profit me $4000. Again it just all depends on the negotiating process with any given store. In some cases I was able to sell that same amount for $15 each! That would be $6000 gross profit. The net profit would be minus the amount paid to the actress's and cost of video cassette "production packaging" (discusses later). However, remember that this figure of $6000 is only one business contact for just one film. This one deal alone took a simple phonecall to open and close. The films were sent and I collected nicely. Now imagine closing 10 deals of that size in 4 weeks.

Place special Concentration on the larger video stores chains. Those store chains are Boardwalk & Park Place. Again, research the business directory at your local library. This directory is usually located in the **reference section**. This directory may list the chains yearly gross revenue. Since this book cannot be checked out (most places), write down names of companies with their telephone numbers. If the company's directory listing does not mention the kinds of films they carry, call the headquarters and ask if they carry adult orientated films? If they do, give them a brief description of yourself and business. Have pencil and paper handy at all times when making your calls. Keep a calendar close by. If they carry adult films in their stores, ask for their sales representative (buyer). Again, keep everything brief at first. You do not want to come across as overly anxious. If the sales rep or buyer seems interested, keep talking. This talking could be more about your business or your interest in their stores. If the buyer doesn't seem interested, this again is when you tease them with a sample video of your film to send. Any deals you have closed with other stores, mention that as well (besides the price). Tell that particular company how other stores including their competition have expressed positive interest in your product. If this doesn't faze them, mention a better deal over their competition. **Of course that's what you want them to think.** Also, you could offer them a further deal, with any new upcoming film products you may have in the future. Again, propose the best deals only to stores with the most outlets (video chains). If this store was a single mom & pop store, you should not have to negotiate that deep. Many chains will claim they have no room for your film/films in their stores. First and foremost none of their claims are written in stone. In fact, nothing is ever written in stone. Negotiating will cover any uncertainties they may have. You want to keep the ball moving and at a steady pace. The biggest mistake would be to offer them (stores, chains) too much to soon. That is a big mistake. Sometimes many of these same stores will give in with just a few minutes of negotiating. Do not give them too much right at first. Bring them in closer and even closer if the negotiation requires it. There have been some cases where the deal seemed impossible to close at first impression. The store claimed they had no room for any more products. I brought the price down just $1 per film, and they gave in. That's what I mean by little at a time. If I had jumped at bringing my price down $5 right at first, that would have been a lot of money lost. When I have to, I will bring the price down greatly, but they are going to have to make me work for it. This also has a lot to do with whom I am talking to. Major chains are the stores you really want to concentrate on. Major chain video stores generate many millions over each year. You want to be where the action and money are taking place. Again, that it the key to making millions in this business. Let's just say for example you only made one deal with one major chain. This amount alone could easily keep you from working your day job (if you chose). The greatest thing is, this one deal could be made within moments of making the phone call.

Will foreign markets offer the same Benefits in terms of chain stores?

Yes, absolutely. Foreign markets offer much opportunity. The key with any market is to identify where the action is taking place. Many individuals think they have to reinvent the wheel in order to make a successful product sell. This is very far from the truth. Just as the adult video market has been proven here in the United States, it will continue to prove even more abroad. Many people think if a product is over saturated it won't sell. This also, is very far from the truth. You can give your film product a further edge in quality that the others lack. If you think something lacks in any particular product, chances are thousands of people feel the same way.

I'll say it again; adult movies with trashy unattractive women have very short shelf lives. Overall these films do not make money. People want to see attractive natural innocent women having lustful sex. People want to see women who would not fit the type of someone to do lustful acts on film. The foreign markets especially love to see women of high nature in appearance doing lustful sex acts.

When one calls a video store or distributor, what could they Expect?

When you talk to the stores buyer, usually you can expect someone friendly and willing to listen to you. Sometimes you will however come across someone who is rude. If this happens the worse thing to do is to tell him or her off. The tendency to do that will be strong, but by any means avoid going off on anyone. That individual could be having other unknown difficulties. Some of the buyers I have talked to in the past, who were rude to me, actually bought the most films. If I had gone off, it would have costed me a lot of money. Another thing was this individual turned out not to be a bad person afterall. Many people are just under so must stress that it leaks through onto others. These people simply do not mean or intend on causing any harm whatsoever. If you come back at someone harshly, they will become very defensive. If you come back at them nicely, they will lighten up and usually apologize for being rude. I have built many relationships with these types of individuals. They have made my income skyrocket. Without them my total income would be cut by at least a 1/4. Remember, you and your business are deemed highly professional. Going off on someone makes you look unprofessional. If your trying to get their business, at least wait 'til your off the phone to let off any steam.

When starting out, it's fun to have that freedom to say whatever to anyone without worrying about reporting to someone else. That freedom is there and does make the job more enjoying. However, when the other person has a checkbook with your name made payable, it's not too wise to lose their business. When it means losing money, it's best to let some things slide. Now if someone gets extremely rude and uses bad language towards you, tell them you don't appreciate it and demand to speak to their boss. When you mention the word "boss", they will get the point. You're not in the position to lose your job **(you are your own boss)**, but they could lose theirs. After that, expect some very special treatment. That's how you handle any situation of that kind. Handling situations that way does not endanger your future business or better yet, **your bank account!**

What if the video store refuses an offer of a sample movie?

If the sample teaser doesn't help, and they happen to be a major chain, bring down your price even more. Right before it gets to the point of losing money, stop negotiating. Thank them for there time and follow up once again with a call back. Remember that you have **nothing to lose**. By calling back, you have everything to gain. Most large video chains have more than one buyer. The buyer that turned you down, might not be the same buyer you talk with today. The second buyer you talk with may be more interested in your films. Never mention to a different buyer that you talked with someone else there before. You don't want to mention you were turned down by someone else at that chain. If you tell them this, they could postpone any progress you have made with them then and there. Also, if they know you talked with someone else they can pick back off with your last negotiating price. This could cost you large amounts of money from being made. That's why it is so important to keep accurate records with everyone you have talked with. That way you will know exactly who you talked with, what the circumstances were like, whether or not you were able to close the deal, if this store is a callback, and the date. When you go to make the callback, you should know the name of the person that turned you down before anyone picks up. Whenever someone picks up on a callback and they introduce themselves with a different name, act like it's the first time you have ever called. This will start the negotiating back at the higher price. Again, do not tell them you were turned down before or that you called before. Now if that person who takes your call on the call back is the same person, start negotiating again regardless. Start negotiating high again, this person could have forgotten the previous conversation. What I recommend doing, is calling the headquarters before you start any negotiating, and find out how many buyers the chain has. This way you will know up front ahead of time. Like I said some chains have many buyers. Since there is a lot of money at stake, find out the number of buyers before you start negotiating any price. If one buyer turns you down, you have the others to fall back on. That would be the smart way to approach the chain video stores or any distributors for that matter. It's always nice to put the odds of closing the deal in your favor. If you solely depend on negotiating with just one buyer, your chances will be much lower.

How many different films will outlets Buy all at once?

Video outlets (stores) will buy as many different films you have. This is especially true when you have sold to them before and your films have already been proven to sell. After you have made a handful of films, further negotiate to get them all into the same stores. This will mean higher profit for you. For instance, if you were to make a $10 profit for each individual film you made, imagine the possibilities of twenty different films with a quantity of 600 each? That is tremendous profit. That's exactly how many top film producers make there multi-millions. It will take a little time to reach the 20 or 30-film amount, but profits can come extremely fast, from just one or two films in the beginning. There are some cases where a single film, outsold 8 or 9 **combined**! Again, make a film that turns you on, promote it, and most important have fun with it.

The most successful people in the world are the ones who love what they do. They <u>made</u> the choice to pursue it. That decision could determine your fate, between clocking into a job you hate, or you watching 2 nude ladies sun bathe on your new boat. Take it from me, the second choice is much better. Make the right choice.

There are 3 types of people in this world. Ones who watch things happen. Ones who wondered what just happened. And the ones who make things happen. Trust your own instincts. Your instincts are far greater than any knowledge available in the world. Remember that.

How can one find business telephone numbers for international outlets?

Some libraries carry an international business directory. This directory will more than likely be in the reference section. This book should be able to provide you with phone numbers (could be expensive to call), addresses, and better yet e-mail address (easier). For international companies, I would contact them by regular mail or e-mail at first. If you don't mind paying for the phone call, give then a call. Foreign markets such as European outlets may require more negotiating, but love sample teasers. Asian markets are also excellent foreign outlets. This market in particular is very geared towards natural looking actresses in the films they purchase.

Tidbit* Asian markets love blondes with fair skin. This part of the world actually places more value on pale white skin, as compared to tan skin. Here in the United States it's the complete opposite. In any U.S. city, you can't drive down the street without seeing a tanning bed business. In Japan, locating a tanning bed can be like searching for Jimmy Hoffa.

The European and Asian markets are the top two regions in terms of foreign distribution. When the time comes to move your films overseas, make these two regions the first.

Where do you go to have your films Reproduced and Packaged?

To have your films mass produced and packaged you will have to use a "duplicating service". There are many businesses's that will copy or duplicate as many films as you need. They will also mass-produce the box covers and packaging for your films. Furthermore, this type of business will also design your movie box to your specifications. What I usually do, is take the Polaroid snapshots (same day as the original filming). Then later on, I hand them over to this service and inform them how I want these pictures to appear on my box cover. The Polaroid snapshots are the pictures you take of the girls the day you film. It takes about 2 to 3 minutes to get some nice pictures of the actresses posing. This posing will be very important. Remember, these pictures are going to be displayed on your movie (box) cover. This is the <u>first thing</u> a potential customer will see, when deciding to rent/buy your film. This is a large part of your marketing package. **Very, very important to get the right snapshots with the woman or women posing.** Again, one of my favorite poses is having a <u>simple</u> shot of a sweet young woman sitting on a bed, wearing something sexy and semi revealing. I would then place this snapshot on the front cover of my movie box. On the back of your movie box, have similar poses printed upside down (so the customer has to look twice).

Selecting your Video duplication Service?

Avoid duplicators that pledge to always offer the lowest price. If you count on packaging and labeling, be certain it is included with the <u>final</u> price quoted. Rush charges may only apply to "same day" assistance.

Things to notice with each duplication service's

Look for full time customer service help. Sales people are often unavailable, but dedicated Customer Service staff should be there when you need them. Remember to ask for an after hours phone number as well. Facilities that operate around the clock will often provide after hour's contact.

Adequate Equipment?

Ask how many duplication machines are on premises?

How many are fully functional?

What's the maintenance schedule like?

Is maintenance service performed <u>on site or off</u>? ***Professionally maintained pieces of equipment will provide higher quality copies of your adult film product.**

Is there an in house tape or **equipment analyzer**? These analyzers improve and maintain quality control, by providing specific information about tape head specifications, drop out rates, and so on. Very few duplication services own such an expensive piece of machinery (Equipment/Tape Analyzer).

Tapestock?

Does the duplicating company load their own cassettes or purchase them commercially?

What is the quality of the tape? Is the tape factory **fresh** at the time your project is duplicated, or was the cassettes loaded months ago and purchased at a clearance price?

The Stability?

How long has the duplicating service been in business? Longevity shows customer devotion, and financial stability.

How do you find Video Duplication companies or Services?

I have included a "Duplication Service Index" on the next several pages for you. I've only had the pleasure to work with some of the companies, but in the index I have provide hundreds of listings for you. Each company could vary in many ways, for better or worst. Some change business policies more often than others.

The people who work and run these types of businesses are wonderful people. They are extremely patient with any needs you may have. They will give you price quotes and special package rates. If something isn't packaged right, most will do whatever it takes to give you what you want.

How many copies of my first film should I have Duplicated from the start?

This is one of the biggest mistakes newcomers have made (including myself in the early days). Never start out by having too many films duplicated without having that number of sales to fall back on. I would start out by having the films duplicated as they are sold. When you sell 200 films for example, call up the duplicating service and have the order sent then. When you find your duplicating service, you can send a copy of each film once you become more established. That way, when large orders come, they will already have your tape to duplicate from. Which will make it easier to pay them, since you could write them a check once a month instead of every other day. When your orders start to roll this will save you time and prevent you from wearing out your checkbook.

How much money do these companies charge for duplication?

The rates for having your tapes duplicated can vary anywhere from two dollars per tape and on up. Most services have special plans, which offer certain price breaks and bargains. Again, each duplicating service will have their own unique packages. The price on duplication depends especially on the number of tapes you plan to have duplicated. For instance, if you have 200 tapes duplicated, you will spend less per tape as compared to having 20 duplicated. To find the right service, compare package prices. Always remember to ask what these packages include. One package from a company may be to high in price, but in turn, could throw in special <u>graphic enhancing</u> for your film box.

Always ask about hidden charges up front. Always make certain that the final price quote is what it says. Some companies will tell you a price, then when it comes time for you to pay, will indicate special charges you were not aware of beforehand. **Get that final price**. After any quote, make 100% certain that's the final price. Again, write down all names (their sales rep).

Keeping accurate records with all businesses will make you life much easier.

Duplicating services and adult films

Most duplicating services will work with adult video material. Some may turn you down, but there are many that won't. You should not have any problems finding someone to duplicate your film. For these duplicating services, this is money out of their pockets if they turn you down. So most will work with you.

If the duplication business is located out of town, do I mail the promotional pictures to them?

If the business is out of town, yes, mail the promotional pictures to the business after you have agreed to have their services **(your hiring them)**. Again, make absolute certain you have the person's name there. **The one who will receive the pictures.** On the envelope, put "Attention--there name". If you forget to put the name of the person, then someone else will have a happy surprise.

Since the pictures you are sending are of extreme importance, go to a local/private film shop with the negatives and have the pictures reproduced. Remember, these snapshots are the pulling force of your film box cover. Without them, your marketing does not exist.

Having extra copies of your pictures (ex. snapshots of a woman posing) is critical, since you can never fully count on getting those pictures back from the duplicator. That's why it's a complete must to have copies made. If you were to do business with another duplication service, you would need them. After you send your pictures to any duplication service, ask them to call you once the pictures arrive. This is for **confirmation** that they received the pictures, and nothing was lost. If your snapshots got lost in the mail for some reason, without the confirmation, the duplication service will think you didn't send them. Then at the same time your wondering what's taking <u>them</u> so long. Before you know it, two or three weeks have gone by. A total waste of time, that could have been avoided with 1 easy phone call.

What if the duplicating company does not call you back, even after you asked them to? If you haven't heard from them six days after your mailing, **call them**. Never wait 2 to 3 weeks. Six days is plenty of time, for confirmation that your snapshots arrived safely.

What kind of graphic enhancement will the duplicating services offer or include in their packages?

The graphic enhancements could be brighter colors and clearer photographs on the front of your movie box cover. Sometimes with Polaroid snapshots the pictures once copied, can at times be on the blurry side. Photo enhancement is almost a must to ensure top rate clear pictures on your box cover. Usually this feature is included with package deals. In my opinion, companies should not abuse this service since it's interest to make quality work. In some cases, extra time is needed to make your snapshots even better.

Graphic enhancement will also help bring out colors in your title heading. This is almost a must. You want your title heading to be full of bright to semi bright colors. Having your colors highlighted will keep your title heading from being dull. If your title heading colors are dull, it will have less effect on catching the customer's eye. Remember, when someone walks into an adult video room, there will be many tapes to choose from. With a bright heading color and a catching photograph on your front box cover, the customer will take great interest. Having a quality film is important, but the quality of your box cover is just as important. Without an appealing box cover, the customer will never know how good your film was, the one they just missed out on.

What colors do I use for my Title Headings?

From past experience, neon blue and hot pink had the best curiosity pulling power. For background colors, black or white is all you need. A great color match would be a neon blue title heading with a black background.

I would highly recommend keeping your credits to the bare minimum on the front cover. The only credit I would place on the front cover would be your title position (producer), along with your name (or stage name). An Example of a title heading (TH) could be:

(Th)-> PRODUCER JOHN DOE BRINGS YOU
~HOT TAN VIXENS WHO DO IT ALL~

sub-heading→ "Bring the lotion and the girls will do the rest"

<Your snapshot photo would go here>:

Copyright info would go here (Use small font)

If your not satisfied with the package design or layout will the duplicators charge a small fee if you decide to cancel?

If you are not happy with the design/layout of your box cover, most duplicators will not charge you. **Always ask about cancellation fees, before you give any duplication service your** business. Before you have any copies of your box made, have the duplicating service make one sample copy for you. Then have them send it to you for personal inspection. This will make their lives easier too. If that sample box cover passes your personal inspection, have the duplicators start your video tape reproduction process.

Should someone have a stage name when Entering the adult film business?

With me personally, yes I would recommend having a stage name. Having a stage name will only protect you. Most stage names are subtle and some are very descriptive. I would pick a stage name that wasn't too blunt but had offered some of flavor.

I know what you're thinking, is Ray West your real name? Yes and no. When I was born, I was not given the West part of the name. The name " Ray West" together was strictly my adult film producer/director name. The last name I have chosen comes from my love of the American west/western movies. My first name Ray, is my real name.

Having a stage name will protect your identity. Believe it or not, some banks will not offer loans to anyone associated with pornography. A great example would be from a scene in "Boogie Nights". If you ever apply for a loan, having that stage name will help protect you. Once you put your real exact name on that box cover, you could invite troubles. Also, if you ever apply for a loan and someone asks occupation, put down film distributor.
Technically you're telling the truth. A distributor is anyone who moves (sells) to other outlets (retail). If they ask for the types of

films you market, do not mention X-rated or Adult. Instead, mention drama or action. Technically this is true. **Watching 2 girls kiss in a hot tub is action/drama** - It's really none of their business, but then again you are asking for their loan (their money).

*Another tip. If you ever have to apply for a loan, and you are asked that same question, **"What type of films do you market"?** Instead of saying action or drama, you can also tell the bank you market <u>documentary films</u>. **Technically you are telling the truth.**

If you have not yet seen the movie Boogie Nights, I highly recommend renting it sometime. A truly remarkable peek into the world of adult films during the late 1970's-early80's. I rarely endorse films publicly, but this one you must see.

<u>Should you make an actress or actor pick a different name before starring in an adult film?</u>

Yes absolutely. Make them pick a different name. Most will arguably agree. They will obviously understand, plus they will have fun creating different names. Now if they are taking all day, to pick a name on the day of shooting, tell them to hurry up and pick one. This should not take all day. In the past, I had three particular girls on the set, and they literally argued over names among themselves for twenty minutes. I was like ok, lets make the film then you can have more time to think of a name. I usually prefer the actresses to have their minds made up concerning stage names before filming. Because all through the filming, the only thing you see is this concentrated thinking face. That's the last thing you want to see in your movie. Instead you want to see the actress in lustful passion, not her without her thinking cap on. That's why I prefer to have the stage names decided on before filming. Most however, come up with their stage names rather quickly.

How long should the average adult film be?

The average adult film is 75 minutes long. If your film is shy of 75 minutes, that is fine. However, I do not recommend making a film less than 60 minutes long. Having a short film will not help your sales whatsoever.

It's also important to put the **film running time** on your movie box cover (somewhere on the front). Never appear to be holding something back from the consumer. Always mention the running time of your film. This does sound obvious, but there are numbers of films without running time mention.

Is there any particular time of year where adult videos sell better?

The adult industry thrives at any time. However, rentals/sales have been known to peak a little higher during the summer. No one really knows exactly why, but during the winter months there have been high peaks as well. It's the one industry that does extremely well anytime and practically anywhere. What makes the adult industry tick is the number of casual buyers/renters. There are numbers of customers who buy/rent on a regular basis. The average price to rent an adult video is $4.25 per night. In most cases, this is more than any mainstream Hollywood new release! With an endless supply of people willing to pay you for it, over and over again. **The people who want to see your movie are constantly looking for <u>you</u>.**

Have you ever noticed what video stores do with films that are not renting well? You can usually find them in a bin or small basket with high mark downed prices. It's the stores way of regaining some money. I often check through these baskets, and it's essentially the same kind of low quality films. Films with terrible looking models and terrible box covers. All of my favorites still remain on the shelves. Very rarely do I find a great box cover with an attractive model sitting in the discount basket. If your local video store has a reduced price basket, take your time to look through it sometime and observe the types of movies that fill it.

<u>Once a store decides to purchase films, how long does the overall process take, from collecting payment and having films duplicated/mailed?</u>

The time it takes the entire process, could be anywhere from 3 days to 4 weeks. This all depends on the size of the order. The duplicating service that your doing business with, has a lot to do with the time process. Some duplicators will drop ship your videos directly to your customers. Once an order is made to you, all you have to do is contact the duplicator and the tapes are sent from there to your customer (ex. video stores). If a video duplicator dropships, make sure the shipping label includes **your** business name & any contact information. As easy as it sounds, there is a disadvantage concerning drop shipping. One of those disadvantages is relying on faith, that the duplicator is getting the shipments out on time. The one good thing about shipping yourself is that you know it got done (shipped to your customers or store buyers). The last thing you want is angry large chain video stores. There have been stories of dropshipping duplicators, not sending the shipment of films to stores until six months after the fact! That does not happen often, but shipping on your own will save you much worry. When stores pay for your product, they want them on the shelves fast.

Another disadvantage with dropshipping is the extra high fees for the service. You could be charged an additional two to three dollars for each tape dropshipped. If you have 400 tapes on order, that's $1200.00 less profit for you. Even if you had to hire someone (ex. Temp) to do the shipping, you would still save an enormous amount. That example sets at 400 tapes, when that quantity becomes 4000+; imagine how much money you will be spending for dropshipment. **Hire some temps**. It's much cheaper. They can take care of any time consuming tasks, such as labeling, packaging, and mailing. While your promoting your films over the phone, you can have your temps take your orders to the post office for delivery. Or call the Post Office, and have them send a delivery truck to pick up your orders (if the orders going out are large, do just that).

*Special Tidbit. Hiring <u>temps</u> instead of regular employees eliminates you from having to fill out employee paperwork with the IRS.

A great tip especially for large orders would be to make a confirmation phone call, to inform your customers there shipment is on the way. This builds instant credibility and shows you care. This type of professionalism will keep stores loyal to your business. In the past, I have always made it a point to make confirmation calls to stores I have recently closed a deal with. I make it a crucial point not to put any confirmation call off from being made. Most video stores are usually surprised to receive one. It's because most filmmakers or distributors never make them.

When the video stores called me to place an order, the process could follow like this. They wanted x amount of my film product for x amount dollars. Deal made. I then called the duplicator, told him how many tapes I needed. Six days later I call that very same store and confirm shipment. Deals such as this can close a $20,000 profit. Once you become more established, imagine 15 or more of these per week. It can happen very easily.

Create a film product → Locate the Demand→ Offer your film to the demand→ Have a way to deliver your film to the demand→Collect your payment→**Repeat**

What about advertising costs?

As you may already know, advertising is one of the most expensive aspects of a business-marketing plan. However, it's good news for you the adult video filmmaker, that you will not have to worry about spending large sums on advertising. Since the market demand is so great, you can rest assure that your advertising costs will be extremely low. One of the only charges you will probably have to pay for in terms of promoting will be the phone bill. Forget about running ads in newspapers (adult) at $75 a day for 1" columns. All you need is a phone and some video stores to contact. Newspaper ads are bridges to possible customers. But direct phone calls to the video store headquarters puts you right there at the pulse.

Now, some people might say "that's just telemarketing, what a crock". But there are major differences between that statement and my statement.

#1. Your list of video stores and distributors to contact are **business related not residential**. There's a big difference between the two. You will **never** have to call someone's home, and say " hey MR. & Mrs. So and so, would you like to see a movie where I have sex with 2 red heads?" Now if you called my home with that offer, I would ask you "who do I make the check out to?" Moving on....

#2 Your list of video stores to contact are targeted. **Micro Soft and GM target business contacts?** That's business. As I mentioned earlier, the power of such tools like the telephone are overly abused each ticking second. By all means, it's not the only tool suffering. Look at the Internet. A tool so powerful and advanced, but at the same time it's loaded with SPAM. Something that was not targeted or requested by the receiving end. If someone requests information, then it's ok to send them mail.

Back to Advertising Discussion....
The only time you would probably pay for advertising space (running an ad) is when you search for talent to star in your video/videos. Aside from that, your advertising costs should be extremely low. If you do decide to experiment with running high dollar ads, try running a small ad in some of the major adult magazines (Hustler, Penthouse). If you do decide to run small classified ads in those publications expect to pay big bucks. Very expensive. I have only ran high dollar ads a few times to test results, and I will say it rarely brings back profits. Most of the time I just broke even. If you decide to run an ad anyway, to gain marketing sales, try to keep the ad three lines or shorter with a strong headline (HOT TAN VIXENS DO IT ALL, example).

Making your opening letter" Personal"?

When you decide to contact video stores or distributors by mail, create a simple opening letter on a separate sheet of paper with your sales message attached. Since the receiving end of your mailing, can't hear your voice, make your opening letter "very personal". Most business letters dull and tiring to look at. By making your **opening letter** personal, your reader (video stores, distributors) can automatically feel comfortable with you from the very beginning, with a strong willingness to read further. The biggest problem with first time mailings is they are often thrown away after the first two lines are read. When a letter is personal it makes the reader feel appreciated. It shows the reader you took the time to write a sincere letter with business interests in mind. This personal letter should not be long at all. **One page** is all you need. Most businesses are extremely busy, anything longer will be thrown away. Your personal letter could start with "Dear Friend" or "Dear, Your Companies name", or that persons name if you know it (might be listed in business directory at local library: reference section). If the name of the individual (buyer/owner) is available in the directory, use their name in the opening of your letter. If you have no name to go by, I would actually recommend using "Dear Friend" in the opening. This opening is friendly and not over used like many others.

Avoid making your letter to-fancy or overwhelming. Letters that are overwhelming cause distractions, which takes away from the actual words.

The layout should be simple but effective. The little things are what matter most.

Choose quality paper. Always include your company letterhead or logo on your opening letter. The letterhead itself does not have to be to fancy, but make sure it's viewable at the **top** of your page.

Avoid any red colors for logos. When someone sees red, it looks too much like a warning.

Keep the paragraphs in your letter short. No more than four sentences per paragraph. **Short paragraphs allow your document to flow smoothly and will hold your readers' interests.**

At the bottom of your opening letter remember to include all personal information for your business.

This would be your name, title, business phone, and address.

The video stores & distributors you will be contacting, gross millions and millions each year. Showing credibility on your personal letter (ex. adding your business logo) gains their confidence in doing business with you.

Include a business card with all business letters. This is quite commonly overlooked. Business cards go a long way. If your letter got lost after being opened, chances are they could still have your business card.

I highly recommend placing a business logo on each of your business cards. Have your logo on anything business related. It's all about credibility. Make the most with everything you send out for your business.

A simple logo believe it or not could actually mean the difference of a major video chain returning your phone call. With that in mind, that could also mean the difference of closing a deal worth

$60,000. **You would not believe now many companies overlook this.**

All businesses can improve sales dramatically by simply placing a simple logo. The purpose again is to build confidence.

At the end of your letter remember to include your own personal signature. This again builds credibility and will make your letter even more personal.

I would also recommend signing your signature with blue ink. By signing with blue ink, it makes the letter appear more authentic. The reason for this is because many letters with black signatures are often copied from machines. With a blue signature it shows that you personally signed it.
Copied business letters with black ink signatures could easily be mistaken for mass mailings.

With this belief, the letter will no longer seem personal. No one likes receiving bulk junk mail, especially businesses.

Always include a date at the top of your letter. This will show that your letter is current and not something used year in & year out.

If you do not hear back from any particular mailings make a follow up call. Follow-ups are crucial.

Use nice envelopes when you start mailing. They do not have to be fancy. Make sure they are large enough so your business letter can easily fit in.

Never write your return address on the envelope with handwriting. This is the one case where personal writing can hurt credibility. Use either printing labels or have your return address stamped on the envelope.

Your Legal Claim Page

This page has to begin at the opening with each film you produce. By federal law the legal claim has to appear. Here is an example of an opening legal claim page:

WARNING

This video/material is intended for a select viewing audience, specifically adults over the age of 21 who view this content instructional and informative purposes only. It is understood that this video/material may not be sold to anyone without clear content. This video may not be exhibited to any minor, nor any individuals who do not wish to view this video/material.

The records required by "Title 18 USC Section 2257 and associated regulations with respect to this video cassette (and all graphical material associated on which this label appears) are kept by the keeper of records at the office of the manufacturer at the following location. The following records contain proof of age, models social security numbers, actual names, aliases, stage names, and or nicknames. Keeper of records:
~PLACE YOUR NAME & BUSINESS ADDRESS HERE~

*Note this name has to be your real name, however its ok to place the first initial of your name followed by your last name. For example, if your name was John Doe, instead of placing John Doe, you could use J. Doe. This still keeps you legal but anonymous.

(Your Company) certifies to all commercial distributors of this video that said materials are in full compliance with the

requirements of Title 18 USC, Section 2257 and related regulations.
Copyright (place year of copyright); (Place company name here) All rights reserved. All models depicted were at least 18 years of age at the time of taping or filming.
(Place the production date here or the day the film was shot.)

More Sources

Adult magazines (Hustler, Penthouse)....

Examine the advertising. Who are the advertisers? Focus on the **benefits** they are selling to the audience. This could help pinpoint further hot buttons in your market. **Treat yourself to some subscriptions.** Hustler and Penthouse are two of my personal favorites.

Extra Sources....

A great reference source is the **Gale's Encyclopedia of Associations** (check local library). This reference source lists all types of U.S. associations. Including addresses and telephone numbers of associations related to any industry.

Another reference source is the **Encyclopedia of Business Information Sources** (check local library). This source also covers industry associations. This source lists trade associations, on-line databases, and books by topic.

Both are from Research, Inc. in Detroit, Michigan and are available at most libraries **(reference section)**.

Copyrights

I highly recommend placing a copyright at the bottom of the opening screen of your movie (after the legal claim page). The fee for a copyright averages $30. To obtain a copyright for your film, write to the below address and request copyright forms for your "video". The forms will be sent to you within a week or so, and will explain the copyright process further. The forms are easy to fill out.

Here's the address to request copyright forms:

THE LIBRARY OF CONGRESS
COPYRIGHT OFFICE
101 INDEPENDENCE AVE,, S.E.
WASHINGTON, D.C. 20559-6000

Your Taxes

Be aware of tax implications when you start your business. This business will be subject to Federal and State taxes. Such taxes may include social security and excise taxes. Also, since you will be the sole proprietor of the business, your personal income tax payments must be prepared on a quarterly basis.

Furthermore, according to the **"Self-Employed Individual Tax Retirement Act"** you can take an income tax deduction considering you set up retirement plans for yourself and for employees you hire (when that time comes).

For more detailed information visit your local office of the Director of Internal Revenue concerning Federal tax obligations.

Upon request they will provide you a very useful booklet (revised yearly), titled **"Tax Guide for Small Business"**.

You will have other State and local taxes. Some more common types of State & local taxes are income, property, sales, and business license. In some states, your not required to pay the fee for a business license until you reach the $10,000 profit earned mark.

For further detailed information concerning your State/local taxes, contact your local state/municipality.

*Tidbit.
Claiming your business as a "Corporation" will protect all your personal assets (such as your home) from any frivolous lawsuit. Your personal property under "Corporation status" is <u>untouchable</u>.

A business classified "Sole Proprietor" does not offer the personal protection of your personal assets.

Since you are just starting out, classify yourself as a "Sole Proprietor". Your taxes will be much lower. With "Corporation status" you will be paying a lot of taxes.

When your business touches the six figure range, go to an accountant, and fill out the "Corporation Status" papers for the IRS. It's that simple to switch. Pay the extra taxes for the added luxury of protection.

Return on Investment

With the adult video business, profits usually far outweigh the initial investment. There are many reasons for this.

First. The adult video does not require a lot of start-up money to make.

Second. The retail or wholesale price can be marked up 10 or more times than the initial cost.

Third. Adult videos have a strong market (very large market).

Fourth. This market is only continuing to grow even bigger, rather than declining.

Fifth. Most businesses require renting or leasing expensive warehouses or store fronts. For instance, a store near a popular mall could cost $70,000 or more to rent a month for space. Having your own adult video business is extremely affordable in terms of your overhead (talent fees, duplicating costs etc). If you have a business with $60,000 overhead, there is a whole lot at stake. **A few poor decisions could easily wipe you out.**

For the adult video business, you can afford to take on anything that tries to set you back. Since the overhead is extremely low, you can afford the flexibility to try many new ideas, without the fear of being shut down in an instant.

Having the freedom of flexibility is a luxury every large or small company lusts for. **And you already have it.**

Plus....
-You have 100% creative control of your business.

-You have 100% control of all business deals.

-You have 100% control of the women you hire for your films. (Not to mention they will be competing for your approval.)

Those statements above are not fantasy but **REALITY**.

People at the top of the adult industry....Where do you think they come from???

Do you honestly think they woke up one morning and was the proud owner of a mansion in the hills with a new Corvette in the driveway?

Please take all the time you want, and read the names below....

Porn legend Ron Jeremy----- was a former school teacher.

The very successful, Ed Powers of "Dirty Debutante" fame---- was at one time a struggling man on the streets of Los Angeles trying to get ahead.

Victoria Paris---worked the regular 9 to 5 office job for many previous years.

Tori Welles '---at one time, was just a stripper in the San Fernando Valley.

Bob Guicione (Publisher of Penthouse magazine)---started his career by enrolling himself in a regular camera class,,,,so he could learn how to photograph nude women. He was literally broke with nothing. He constructed the very first Penthouse magazine with paste, paper, and pictures with his bare hands on his apartment floor!

Luck??? Or Choice???

The list goes on and on……

Asking Questions

Questions are the keys to information, needs, and emotions.

The person asking questions is always in **control**.

This control can lead to long lasting business relationships that will pay handsomely for you many years to come.

Obtaining the Referral

We pass them out each day to friends and even strangers. We respond to a request either direct or implied, with suggestions, phone numbers, cards and any other ways of connecting to people.

Referrals are *bonds* that keep everyone connected.

Can you build business with them? You certainly can. Here are ways you can increase referrals:

Simply Ask: You would be surprised how many people do not. So how do we obtain them? By asking! Oversimplified?

By simply asking a video store for a referral, you will increase your chances of getting a name or two.

This name or two could be a major video chain, wanting your films in each of their stores!

*Don't overlook other businesses (such as duplicators) as tremendous resources for additional referrals. Many have long contacts within the adult market, and can sometimes update you on any current events.

Remember that businesses are all built one contact at a time.

Presenting Voice Mail Messages to Video Stores and Distributors

Voice mail is a fantastic when used correctly. The voice mail message should be to the point. A book unfolds into a story but voice mail should get right to it. Treat voice mail as the 'repetitive' medium. Create a short, high-interest message of benefit to the recipient. Speak slowly with confidence. Clearly state your name, company title, and phone number. Try to include a **hook** or an incentive to grab attention. This hook could be anything from offering a sample video or mentioning the knockout quality of women in your film.

Repeatedly, leave this identical weekly message in the video stores and distributors voice mailbox. You will be contacted. Your prior persistent voice mail messages will have already set the stage for you.

Time: Make it count

Time is of the essence. Time is critical to selling your movies. Time is a limited resource. You have unlimited choices each and everyday. Time can be used or wasted. You can decide what to do with your time, or you can let time dribble by.

No one has control over the speed of time. It cannot be speeded up or slowed down. The control over time is nonexistent. How you use your time represents control.

Success

Again, It's quite simple. Make an adult film you would rent yourself. Because, there are millions of people with similar interests and tastes as **you**. If you enjoy watching threesomes, then odds are millions of other people do to (including me). The adult industry is supremely unique in that everyone enjoys watching or performing sex (**most may not openly admit it**). With that statement,,,,this need will always have to be fulfilled. And there will always be a constant supply of people willing to pay you for it.

Do not sell yourself short

Once you have established the value of your film, present the price with confidence. Never apologize for the price. The willingness to walk away comes from having options.

Focus on the **value** of your movie, not price. Buyers will pay for value. Tell the video stores & distributors you can help them out. If you lack confidence about your adult film product, buyers will become aware of your doubts.

You are Entitled to Compensation

Just as your doctors are entitled to a reasonable compensation for their services, you are entitled to compensation for your adult film products. No buyer will begrudge you a price that is relative to the perceived value of the film product.

Record Keeping

The keeping of accurate records can not be stressed enough. Without organized records, you cannot see in advance which way your business is going.

With an adequate bookkeeping system you can answer such questions as:

-How much business am I doing?

-What are my expenses?

-What's my gross profit? My net profit?

*Simply record the information as they occur.

Negotiating Your Films?

Negotiating is not constant arguing; negotiating is talking, with goal in mind.

Negotiation is not manipulating; negotiation taps into mutual motivation. Negotiating does not need over aggressiveness; negotiating needs assertiveness.

A prepared negotiator assumes everything is negotiable. The answers are always changing. Negotiating helps you get what you want.

Seek "win-win" or mutually beneficial results. This attitude toward life and business, demonstrates your goal to reach mutual satisfying solutions. This attitude enables you to build long lasting relationships with results.

A quick word on relationships....

The approach you take to business determines whether people trust you. With the pace of unexpected change, it's essential to develop lasting business relationships. Relationships are trust. Your sincerity towards your films will motivate other business's to invest their trust & money.

People always extend consideration –to people they like and trust.

Negotiating Your Price

For your adult films, you want to leave yourself the option of a lower price. The principle here is called **"saving face"**. In other words, you will only lower if you can save face, i.e., maintain integrity of your pricing structure.

Tell the prospect (store, distributor etc), "I only accept lower prices under the following circumstances...".

What are the circumstances?

You could offer to reduce the price in return for additional commitment to purchase other film products at full price.

Remember, just because the buyer has a vendor with a lower price does not always mean they want that vendor.

Making the Buyer work

One time a distributor tried to convince me to drastically lower my price, but I politely refused. In the end, the distributor booked me because they later viewed my sample video as worth my original asking price. With a little patience, I closed a very handsome deal.

If you lower the price, make the buyer work for it.

The fear of Negotiating

People resist negotiating for many unknown reasons. A primary reason many people avoid negotiating is because they have been socialized to avoid it. One recent survey shows 70% of all new car buyers never try to negotiate the sticker price!

Another reason, is negotiating requires **patience**. Take the time to understand what motivates the other side. You can create solutions that satisfy both parties needs.

Speaking the language

Ask video stores & distributors what types of publications they read. This will further enable you to relate to them.

The second source is "**Standard Rate and Data Service, Business or Consumer Publications**", available from SRDS in Willamette, Illinois (check your local library). This publication lists many sources by industry and category.

By understanding what you have in common, you can easily communicate with them.

The Seven Points of Prospecting

The "**Seven Points of Prospecting**"....

Point I
Prospecting requires **discipline**. I can assure you the time to prospect will never be exactly right. Make an appointment with yourself each day for prospecting new businesses.

Point II
Before prospecting, you should always take the time to properly target (ex. larger video stores that carry adult films). If you do this, you will concentrate on the best prospects in the market. If you only call the best prospects in the market, every call will be a quality call since they are most likely to buy large quantities of your adult film product.

Point III:

Make your calls brief. The objective of the call is to get the appointment with the buyer (over of phone). Your prospecting call should be focused on introducing yourself, your product, briefly understanding the prospects needs so that you can provide them with a very good **reason** to spend some of their valuable time with you.

Point IV:
Work without interruption. I recommend not taking any unimportant calls during your prospecting time. Take full **advantage** of your prospecting. Often called **"getting in the groove".**

Point V: Try prospecting during off peak hours when conventional times do not work. Conventional cold calling hours fall between 9:00 AM and 5:00 PM. Set aside some time each day during this period to prospect. When conventional cold calling hours are not working, consider supplementing your prospecting time during off peak hours.

Point VI:
Get organized. Keep documented notes after each contact, along with dates and names. Your **goal** is to get the buyer.

Point VII:
Do not stop. **Persistence** is the special virtue in <u>selling success</u>. Some of the largest deals are made after the fifth call. **Most people quit after the first.**

Talking Versus Listening

What does talking and listening have in common when it comes to overall selling? The unusual connection here is that most people do too much of one and not enough of another.

Most people overlook listening when they sell. But great salespeople are all great **listeners**.

Some listening hints....

-Listen for answers to revealing questions. This, of course, means asking questions that are targeted and directed to help your prospect **define** how you can help them.

-Never interrupt the prospect. Be ready to be interrupted, but never interrupt, or curb what your prospect is saying.

-Concentrate on what the prospect is saying. Don't focus on what they are going to say. Listen with each sentence, one at a time. Never assume what they'll say next.

-Paraphrase what you are hearing. Ask questions to verify. By verifying, you **match** what they really mean.

-Clarification. Never be afraid to ask, "What do you mean by that?" or "Could you explain?" Be 100% sure of what is being communicated.

-Feedback. This will prove that you fully understand what the prospect is saying and how it is intended.

-Listen with your heart and ears. Listen for the tone, speed and intent of your prospect's comments. Not just for information alone.

-Summarize. Repeat back to the prospect your understanding. Then verify that your understanding is correct.

The next time you make a purchase, observe the salesperson. How much do they talk in comparison with listening? How many questions do they ask? How frustrated are you when not given the opportunity to tell them what you really want or need?

The bottom-line. You can listen your way into greater video sales than you can talk yourself into----everytime.

Using the Reflective Communication Method

Let's look at one aspect of listening – **reflective communication**. This is when you repeat someone's words back in question form. This method works especially well when contacting video stores to get sales. For example, a prospect may say, "I love baseball." Your response, **"Baseball? What do you love about baseball?"** Or your prospect may say, **"Customer service is terrible at most places.** Then you can respond, **"Terrible? Why do you feel it's terrible?"**. This method makes the prospect feel understood. Plus, it doesn't sound like you have a script or secret agenda. If you use reflective listening, your prospects (distributors and video stores) will happily tell you <u>everything</u> you want to know.

More prospecting Tips

Avoid wasting the prospect's time – Quickly start on the issues as soon as the prospect chooses to do so. Tell the prospect what you'd like to accomplish.

Asking the right questions – Questions concerning any problems, challenges, or goals. Record all answers.

Suggesting the correct solution – Present solutions that relate solely to the prospects buying reasons for your adult films.

Let the prospect make the purchase – you do not have to pressure a prospect in order for them to buy from you. Remember, prospects buy for **their reasons**, not yours.

Some Questions to play with

15 minutes is what percent of a twenty-four hour day?

15 minutes is what percent of an eight-hour day?

How many minutes in a day?

How many hours in a week?

Average life expectancy for a male/ female?

Amount of time you have left?

Most people do not have a clue to the answers because they macro-manage their time. Macros waste a lot of time. The micro's keep track with things they do and typically get more done. The difference between the two is small yet large at the same time. It's small since minor changes are easy to adopt. It's large, which could be staggering to your schedule but could <u>dramatically change your life forever.</u>

Some more useful hints....

- Your calendar is the center of your life. Identify what's important and put those things on your calendar.

- Place time cushions in your schedule each day. A little elasticity goes a long way.

- Always ask yourself each day "Is there a better way?" If you find a better way, make the necessary changes.

- When you become more established, avoid doing anything if someone else can do it for you. You can't increase your sales if you're doing a lot of non-selling chores. The highest priority is marketing your films.

The answers....

15 minutes is 1% of a full day.

15 minutes is 3% of an 8-hour day of work.

There are 1440 minutes in a 24-hour day.

168 hours in a week.

Never put off living. "Life is short and no one has ever gotten out alive."

Two important Traps to avoid

-Never settle on a single idea. Ideas are the currency of business success. Brainstorm and use as many ideas to see which ones bring more profits and success.

-If an idea fails. Learn, and move on to newer ones.

Choice of words

Some Phrases to Avoid During Your Sales Message:

We are the best in the business.

Is price important?

Tell me what you think?

When will you make the decision?

We are price competitive

I see your point

When will you let me know?

Can I call you in a couple weeks?

Are you having any problems?

I do not know.

We cannot do that.

Hang on a sec

It's our policy

What do I have to do?

So, tell me what you think?

First I need you to…

You will have to…

I happen to be wondering

I think maybe

How soon do you need?

I'm not exactly sure

So what's going on?

I completely guarantee it.

I have got to be straight with you

Reacting to Objections

The most popular time to react is when we feel the sale is being threatened. This will usually occur in the beginning or during the end of the sales presentation.

For a moment, imagine you are at the end of your sales presentation with a large video chain. You then hear the six words; "I want to think about it." Often enough, the salesperson will react to that statement with the first word being **BUT:**

BUT our service is,

BUT it's a great price,

BUT we have the best,

BUT we will do a good job,

After the objection, the salesperson becomes confused and reacts because they feel the sale is <u>threatened</u>. So they **dump** the information on the prospect. This unfortunately, comes across as being overly defensive. Usually when someone is over defensive, it's done through a show of force. After that happens, a wall has been created, and any active listening has been <u>diminished</u>.

Ineffective salespeople react by defending what they have said and they try to convince the prospect that what they are feeling is wrong.

For example, when the prospect says, "I need to think about it", or makes a statement such as, "too high," what they say, is usually not what they mean.

When someone expresses an objection, we aren't fully sure what information they are still <u>looking</u> for. Yet, many people often act as if they already know. They dump useless information. Often, the answer is two to three questions deep. The professional must peep **behind** words that describe how the person on the other end is feeling.

When you hear an objection that's preventing the prospect from making a purchasing decision, learn to respond with a question to <u>uncover</u> the true reason that's preventing the sale. Doing this, will save you needless wasted effort and will produce more profitable results.

The professional knows how to reply with a question.

Some Questioning examples are as follows

-What do you feel is missing?

-Is it possible to have another solution here?

-Could you share with me, why you see it that certain way?

Responding with questions will provide solutions to what they want, not the ones you think.

Your Goals

The only goals you will get really excited about are your own.

When you set goals, you predict your future. When you create plans, you define the future. <u>And when you act, you make your future.</u>

Take time to thank your clients and prospects

Do it in person, via phone or with a hand written note.

The Most Important

If you remember just one thing from this book, remember this next sentence faithfully. Always, and always practice <u>safe sex</u>!!! Never assume nothing will happen to you if you choose not to do so. You do not need me to tell you how serious Aids is. This disease however in certain places is declining thankfully, but it's full effect in the world remains very strong. Before anything else mentioned in this book, take this paragraph to heart. Always wear a condom!!! No matter what the circumstance. Also, before you hire or pay any models, have them bring back a current HIV and Herpes test result. Always check the date on any test results along with the models real name and social security number. Make sure everything from the test result matches with the models vital statistics. After all safety considerations have been met, I'll see you at the ballgame!

Video Duplicating Service Index

The following index lists video-duplicating services you can use. Keep in mind that some of these companies **change** policies and may offer more than others. **Always compare price packages from each company.** Since you are just starting out, my advice would be to start with a low minimum tape stock or supply. Once your sales begin to dramatically increase, then order your films in larger supply.

In the beginning.... sell as you go!

Video Imaging
951 West Pipeline Road, Fort Worth, TX 76161
(817) 590-2030

Video Workshop Inc
6001 San Mateo Boulevard, Albuquerque, NM 87109
(505) 888-2433

Video Visions
9712 Candelaria Road, Albuquerque, NM 87112
(505) 292-8365

Vaughn Duplication Services
3694 Westchase Drive, Houston, TX 77042
(713) 266-4269

Video Factory
3800 Carlisle Boulevard, Albuquerque, NM 87107
(505) 881-7878

Video Tape It
2111 Menaul Boulevard, Albuquerque, NM 87107
(505) 888-2848

Video One
2760 North Grandview Avenue, Odessa, TX 79762
(915) 362-7943

Accent Video
2294 East Dorothy Lane, Dayton, OH 45420
(937) 299-6400

Video Mart
804 North White Sands Boulevard, Alamogordo, NM 88310(505) 434-4548

A V S Productions
Maple Heights, OH 44137
(216) 663-5910

Capital Video Services
1406 Luisa Street, Santa Fe, NM 87505
(505) 982-9221

Video Magic
2620 North 11th Street, Beaumont, TX 77703409) 899-2960

4 JS Video Production
Hanford, CA 93230
(559) 582-6323

Hollinger Video Productions
(334) 265-8555

5 Stars Photo Studio
5332 Geary Boulevard, San Francisco, CA 94121
(415) 831-9990
A & A Enterprises
North Hollywood, CA 91601
(818) 985-6424

Aavid Video Service
814 Morena Boulevard, San Diego, CA 92110
(619) 291-5205

Bertsch Video Productions
Santa Ana, CA 92701
(714) 557-9522

Gosch Production
5144 Vineland Avenue, North Hollywood, CA 91601
(818) 509-3530

Plus Discount Video Service
450 South Central Avenue, Glendale, CA 91204
(818) 956-1444

A To Z Video Taping
Lomita, CA 90717
(310) 539-6336

A B Duplication
2139 Tapo Suite # 109, Simi Valley, CA 93063
(800) 838-6691

A Digital House Productions
2605 Camino Del Rio South, San Diego, CA 92108
(619) 299-2850

Plum Video Productions
13428 Maxella Avenue Suite 611,Marina DelRey,CA 90292 (310) 398-2390

Tamayo Video Productions
1539 West Magnolia Boulevard, Burbank, CA 91506
(818) 843-3188

A-1 Cassette Duplication
714 C Street, San Rafael, CA 94901
(415) 459-4048

A-1 Video Warehouse
On Blck Of Wshngtn South, Fremont, CA 94536
(510) 656-3100

AAA Duplication
1200 Concord Avenue, Concord, CA 94520
(925) 687-3750

AAA Video Service
467 North Tustin Street, Orange, CA 92867
(714) 538-6830

Access Video Productions
841 Gilman Street, Berkeley, CA 94710
(510) 528-6044

Advanced Duplicating Services
Studio City, CA 91604
(661) 288-1650

Advanced Video Duplication
6922 Hollywood Boulevard, Los Angeles, CA 90028
(323) 466-1363

Daily Video Services
3306 West Burbank Boulevard, Burbank, CA 91505
(818) 556-6386

Dalan Productions
18464 Ward Street, Fountain Valley, CA 92708
(714) 964-3903

Davis S R Productions
1295 Boulevard Way, Walnut Creek, CA 94595
(925) 946-9856

Denevi Video Reflections
21091 Foothill Boulevard, Hayward, CA 94541
(510) 727-8880

Dub City
348 Rose Avenue, Danville, CA 94526
(925) 552-8081

Duplication by Transvideo
990 Villa Street, Mountain View, CA 94041
(650) 965-4898

Duplication Center of America
15870 Bernardo Center Drive, San Diego, CA 92127
(858) 675-9050

Duplication Connection
600 East Franklin Street, Monterey, CA 93940
(831) 373-0493

Duplications Corporation
1045 Sansome Street, San Francisco, CA 94111
(415) 981-0556

East Bay Media Center
1939 Addison Street, Berkeley, CA 94704
(510) 843-3699

Film & Video Transfers Inc
8523 Reseda Boulevard, Northridge, CA 91324
(818) 885-6501

Five Star Conference Recording & Duplicating
Carlsbad, CA 92008
(760) 931-8414

Format Video
PO Box 31538, San Francisco, CA 94131
(415) 681-9774

Full Circle Video Productions
Santa Cruz, CA 95060
(831) 459-8300

Aargil Video Dub
630 9th Avenue, New York, NY 10036
(212) 765-7788

Advanced Media Solutions
New York, NY 10001
(212) 979-8655

Advanced Video Techniques
5500 Main Street, Buffalo, NY 14221
(716) 631-0515

AJ Discount Video
216 Briarwood Drive, Rochester, NY 14617
(716) 336-9890

Al-Art Video Production Limited
144 Bixley Heath, Lynbrook, NY 11563
(516) 887-8422

All IN One Productions Inc
401 Broadway, New York, NY 10013
(212) 334-4778

American Video Service Department
516 Amsterdam Avenue, New York, NY 10024
(212) 724-4870

All Star Video Productions
6 Bush Court, New City, NY 10956
(914) 634-4218

American Video Inc
717 Lexington Avenue, New York, NY 10022
(212) 888-0340

Associated Video Productions
407 Lincoln Road, Brooklyn, NY 11225
(718) 756-5191

Dub Works
630 9th Avenue, New York, NY 10036
(212) 765-7788

Duplication Depot Inc
215 Central Avenue Suite B, Farmingdale, NY 11735
(516) 752-0608

Duplication Specialists Inc
843 Merrick Road, Baldwin, NY 11510
(516) 867-7300

D E R Duplicating Service
214 Northwest 4th Avenue, Hallandale, FL 33009
(954) 458-7505

David Sheriff Video Productions
7025 Beracasa Way, Boca Raton, FL 33433
(561) 394-9652

Dillon Video & Film Productions Inc
2330 Northeast 8th Road, Ocala, FL 34470
(352) 620-0686

Georgia Audio Video Services
4651 Roswell Road Northeast, Atlanta, GA 30342
(404) 843-3616

Dolphin Images
1825 Northeast 149th Street, Miami, FL 33181
(305) 945-6789

JB Productions
3097 Presidential Drive, Atlanta, GA 30340
(770) 458-2708

Dubs Plus Services
625 Lake Osborne Terrace, Lake Worth, FL 33461
(561) 547-5513

4 M Video Productions
3220 West Raleigh Hill, Peoria, IL 61604
(309) 673-4738

Eastern Video Corporation
7111 Biscayne Boulevard, Miami, FL 33138
(305) 759-7111

A B A Video
79 West Monroe Street, Chicago, IL 60603
(312) 853-3456

Daniel Video Productions
Savannah, GA 31401
(912) 897-6695

Abbey Productions
3825 North Elston Avenue, Chicago, IL 60618
(773) 539-5665

Danda Productions
2262 Northwest Southeast, Marietta, GA 30067
(770) 953-4100

Absolute Video Services
715 South Euclid Avenue, Oak Park, IL 60304
(708) 386-7550

Access Video Services Inc
Oak Park, IL 60301
(708) 848-6876

Accurate Video Services
Lake Zurich, IL 60047
(847) 438-1166

Exact Video Duplication
502 Parkside Drive, Carol Stream, IL 60188
(630) 665-3331

HF Productions
206 South Friedline Drive, Carbondale, IL 62901
(618) 457-7649

Infinite Video Productions
1825 Fabyan Parkway, West Chicago, IL 60185
(630) 232-6862
Affordable Video
820 East Westfield Boulevard, Indianapolis, IN 46220
(317) 259-7250

Band Wagon Video Productions
16575 State Road 120 Suite C, Bristol, IN 46507
(219) 848-5969

D J Video
3410 North Wheeling Avenue, Muncie, IN 47304
(765) 284-3380

F 4 Tape CO Inc
Brownsburg, IN 46112
(317) 852-5540

Full Perspective Video
6902 Hawthorn Park Drive, Fishers, IN 46038
(317) 579-0400

Hanley Video Duplication
7717 Castle Ridge Court, Fishers, IN 46038
(317) 577-8220

Anderson Film Service
106 West Broadway, Council Bluffs, IA 51503
(712) 322-6910

Apple Video
8527 University Boulevard, Clive, IA 50325
(515) 279-2500

Copy Rite Video
18341 290th Street, Mason City, IA 50401
(515) 423-3496

EBI Video
5000 Tremont Avenue, Davenport, IA 52807
(319) 391-0619

Infinity Video Services
8218 Plaza Lane, Des Moines, IA 50320
(515) 287-3735

Absolute Duplication Inc
Baton Rouge, LA 70821
(225) 752-2648

Channel One Video Inc.
1300 Bertrand Drive, Lafayette, LA 70506
(337) 234-1422

Creative Video Productions
1373 Aberdeen Avenue, Baton Rouge, LA 70808
(225) 383-7443

Cross Lake Video
5777 South Lakeshore Drive, Shreveport, LA 71119
(318) 635-3581

Fast Forward Productions
120 Representative Row, Lafayette, LA 70508
(337) 234-3348

A AA Video Duplicating & Standards Conversion
Silver Spring, MD 20901
(301) 445-5450

Advanced Duplications
11438 Cronridge Drive, Owings Mills, MD 21117
(410) 363-3706

Allied Film & Video
819 Brightseat Road, Hyattsville, MD 20785
(301) 808-6100

Dubmax Discount Duplicators
Baltimore, MD 21201
(410) 325-5600

King Video Productions
12202 Fingrbrd Road, Monrovia, MD 21770
(301) 831-3500

Markets Video Specialities
4419 East West Highway, Bethesda, MD 20814
(301) 718-2637

Milner-Fenwick Video
2125 Greenspring Drive, Lutherville, MD 21093
(410) 560-1212

On Line Suburban Video Inc
15732 Crabbs Branch Way, Derwood, MD 20855
(301) 548-9181

Professional Video Services
6380 Hanover Crossing Way, Hanover, MD 21076
(410) 796-0848

Professional Video Production Company Inc
Baltimore, MD 21201
(410) 653-8433

Quality Film & Video
232 Cockeysville Road, Cockeysville, MD 21030
(410) 785-1920

Satellite Video Production
8379 Inspiration Avenue, Walkersville, MD 21793
(301) 845-2737

Stonewall Video Productions
4507 Metropolitan Court, Frederick, MD 21704
(301) 695-7181

U-Star Video Productions
Upper Marlboro, MD 20774
(301) 249-0924

Video Ed Productions Inc
4301 East West Highway, Hyattsville, MD 20782
(301) 927-7474

Video On Location
11600 Nebel Street, Rockville, MD 20852
(301) 984-5823

Video Services Company
Elkridge, MD 21075
(410) 379-5620

Video Transfer Inc
5709 Arundel Avenue, Rockville, MD 20852
(301) 881-0270

A To Z Video Service
2908 Main St, Kansas City, MO 64108
(816) 753-2100

Above & Beyond Productions & Duplications Inc
7305 Lindell Boulevard, Saint Louis, MO 63130
(314) 862-6656

American Video Productions
Branson, MO 65615
(417) 338-4323

Branson Video Duplication
420 State Highway 165, Branson, MO 65616
(417) 336-3827

Dub Center
1433 East Sunshine Street, Springfield, MO 65804
(417) 883-0323

Verbatim Video Services
1528 East Glenwood Street, Springfield, MO 65804
(417) 882-0901

Video Clones
1617 Tamarack Drive, Saint Charles, MO 63301
(636) 949-2982

Video Pros
Kansas City, MO 64108
(816) 474-7767

Video Services Group Inc
11126 Lndbrgh Bsns Court, Saint Louis, MO 63123
(314) 487-8045

Videoworx Productions
3715 Beck Road, Saint Joseph, MO 64506
(816) 364-0022

Videogenics
RR 3 Box 3, Joplin, MO 64801
(417) 782-9424

A 1 Video Transfer
Las Vegas, NV 89125
(702) 870-9110

All Around Video Laboratory
886 East Sahara Avenue, Las Vegas, NV 89104
(702) 735-2679

Canyon Video Services
Las Vegas, NV 89117
(702) 257-7477

High Speed Video
6171 McLeod Drive, Las Vegas, NV 89120
(702) 798-2859

Mirage Video Duplication Inc
6760 Boulder Highway, Las Vegas, NV 89122
(702) 362-3827

NTV Productions
5665 South Valley View Bl, Las Vegas, NV 89118
(702) 795-2688

U Edit Complete Video Services
2290 East Flamingo Road, Las Vegas, NV 89119
(702) 731-9441

Transfer West Duplication
6171 McLeod Drive, Las Vegas, NV 89120
(702) 895-9900

Vegas Post & Duplication
721 East Charleston Bl,
Las Vegas, NV 89104
(702) 388-0277

Video Cat Productions
115 West Plumb Lane 208, Reno, NV 89509
(775) 322-3200

The Video Man Productions
Lakewood, NJ 08701
(732) 905-0941

20-20 Video Productions LLC
35 North Middaugh Street, Somerville, NJ 08876
(908) 707-9322

A C P Video Productions Corporation
83 North 8th Street, Hawthorne, NJ 07506
(973) 423-0800

Duplication Services Inc
91 Ruckman Road, Closter, NJ 07624
(201) 768-5005

Easy Video of Plainsboro
10 Schalks Crossing Road, Plainsboro, NJ 08536
(609) 799-9646

Forever Video Limited
30 Tomar Court, Bloomfield, NJ 07003
(973) 338-6641

Highlight Productions LLC
Long Branch, NJ 07740
(732) 229-1250

Video Palace Inc
286 Park Avenue, Rutherford, NJ 07070
(201) 933-3373

DXB Video Tapes of Virginia Inc
Forest, VA 24551
(804) 525-6467

Grissom Production Services Inc
Arlington, VA 22201
(703) 892-1588

Landmark Video Duplication
1909 Huguenot Road, Richmond, VA 23235
(804) 378-8273

Metro Video Productions
8 South Plum Street, Richmond, VA 23220
(804) 359-2500

Dallas Duplicating Service
2414 US Highway 80 East, Mesquite, TX 75149
(972) 329-7092

Dub Express
1603 Babcock Road, San Antonio, TX 78229
(210) 979-7371

Dub King
2565 Jackson Keller Road, San Antonio, TX 78230
(210) 979-8779

Dub King Duplication Service
2105 Justin Lane, Austin, TX 78757
(512) 451-3827

Dubbit
6200 La Calma Drive, Austin, TX 78752
(512) 459-3100

Dynamic Video Productions
1621 Upland Drive, Houston, TX 77043
(713) 722-0111

Angelfire Productions
1 Sweetwater Drive, Prescott, AZ 86301
(520) 445-5050

Arizona Media Duplication
4840 South 35th Street, Phoenix, AZ 85040
(602) 276-7776

Avalon Video Productions
Tucson, AZ 85726
(520) 327-3536

Bold Eagle Productions
405 North Beaver Street, Flagstaff, AZ 86001
(520) 774-7581

Dub City West
2727 West Southern Avenue, Tempe, AZ 85282
(602) 438-8267

Foothills Video Service
Tucson, AZ 85726
(520) 295-1139

Hays House Video Productions
Phoenix, AZ 85018
(480) 947-0488

Jerrys Video Transfer Service
456 West Main Street, Mesa, AZ 85201
(480) 644-0229

K & A Video Duplication
Phoenix, AZ 85028
(602) 787-0272

King Tapes
14 North Robson, Mesa, AZ 85201
(480) 969-2956

Master Duplicating Corporations
Phoenix, AZ 85017
(602) 274-9111

Video Converting Duplicating & Editing
(520) 326-0869

Video Workshop
4585 East Speedway Boulevard, Tucson, AZ 85712
(520) 323-3151

Fox Video
Stamford, CT 06901
(203) 357-8488

Video House Inc
208 Greenwood Avenue, Bethel, CT 06801
(203) 748-0239

Video Production Associates
525 Bridgeport Avenue Suite 10, Shelton, CT 06484
(203) 929-8869

Video Transfer
99 Danbury Road, Ridgefield, CT 06877
(203) 431-3488

Video Film Transfer & Duplicating Laboratory
13251 Northend Avenue, Oak Park, MI 48237
(248) 548-7580

World Video Transfer Service
2007 15 Mile Road, Sterling Heights, MI 48310
(810) 795-8866

D & DS Video Transfer Service
37108 6 Mile Road, Livonia, MI 48152
(734) 591-3660

Heitman Video Services
Elizabeth Court, Mount Pleasant, MI 48858
(517) 775-3399

Vidcam Productions
10683 South Saginaw Street, Grand Blanc, MI 48439
(810) 694-0996

Video Graphics Taping Service
9541 Telegraph Road, Redford, MI 48239
(313) 537-5900

Sunseri Video Productions
1548 Methyl Street, Pittsburgh, PA 15216
(412) 388-1643

Video Cassette Duplication Services
5001 Baum Boulevard, Pittsburgh, PA 15213
(412) 687-5300

Action Duplication Inc
203 Oak Knoll Road, New Cumberland, PA 17070
(717) 770-2550

LA Mode Video Productions
810 Park Way, Broomall, PA 19008 (610) 328-6760

American Duplicating CO
243 Zimmerman Lane, Langhorne, PA 19047
(215) 547-5722

Eyemark Video Services
310 Parkway View Drive, Carnegie, PA 15106
(412) 747-4700

DELP Jay M Video
10 Valley Drive, Telford, PA 18969
(215) 723-6133

Genesis Video Productions
RR 2 Box, New Brighton, PA 15066
(724) 847-4400

Gold Star Video Duplication
725 North 24th Street, Philadelphia, PA 19130
(215) 236-3939

Video Cassette Services
5001 Baum Boulevard, Pittsburgh, PA 15213
(412) 687-5300

Video Copy Center
1112 Mount Rose Avenue, York, PA 17403
(717) 854-8507

Video Gold Productions
1094 2nd Street Pike, Richboro, PA 18954
(215) 322-1428

Advanced Video Productions
2111 Elder Street, Chattanooga, TN 37404
(423) 622-1858

H & W Distributing CO Inc
5640 Summer Avenue, Memphis, TN 38134
(901) 385-8600

Master Video Productions Inc
2572 Jackson Avenue, Memphis, TN 38108
(901) 372-7012

"Spring Break & Las Vegas"

Hotel & Motel Travel Listings

The following list includes:

-Las Vegas, Nevada

-Daytona Beach, Florida

-Fort Lauderdale, Florida

-Padre Island, Texas

-Lake Havasu, Arizona

-Palm Springs, California

Las Vegas
Caesars Palace
3570 Las Vegas Boulevard South, Las Vegas, NV 89109
(702) 731-7110

Las Vegas Hilton
3000 Paradise Road, Las Vegas, NV 89109
(702) 732-5111

Las Vegas Club Hotel & Casino
18 Fremont Street, Las Vegas, NV 89101
(702) 385-1664

LA Quinta Inns
7101 Cascade Valley Court, Las Vegas, NV 89128
(702) 360-1200

Las Vegas Milestone Hotel
1919 Fremont Street, Las Vegas, NV 89101
(702) 387-1650

Las Vegas Marriott Suites
325 Convention Center Drive, Las Vegas, NV 89109
(702) 650-2000

Las Vegas South Travelodge
3735 Las Vegas Boulevard South, Las Vegas, NV 89109
(702) 736-3443

Lone Mountain Buffet at the Santa Fe Hotel & Casino
4949 North Rancho Drive, Las Vegas, NV 89130
(702) 658-4900

Mandalay Bay Resort & Casino
3950 Las Vegas Boulevard South, Las Vegas, NV 89119
(702) 632-7777

Maxim Hotel & Casino
160 East Flamingo Road, Las Vegas, NV 89109
(702) 731-4300

MGM Grand Hotel Casino City of Entertainment
3799 Las Vegas Boulevard South, Las Vegas, NV 89109
(702) 891-1111

New York New York Hotel & Casino
3790 Las Vegas Boulevard South, Las Vegas, NV
89109
(702) 740-6969

New Frontier Hotel & Casino
3120 Las Vegas Boulevard South, Las Vegas, NV
89109
(702) 794-8200

Nevada Palace Hotel & Casino
5255 Boulder Highway, Las Vegas, NV 89122
(702) 458-8810

Orleans the Hotel & Casino
4500 West Tropicana Avenue, Las Vegas, NV 89103
(702) 365-7111

Palace Station Hotel & Casino
2411 West Sahara Avenue, Las Vegas, NV 89102
(702) 367-2411

Paris Las Vegas
3655 Las Vegas Boulevard South, Las Vegas, NV

89109
(702) 946-7000

Queen of Hearts Hotel
19 Lewis Avenue, Las Vegas, NV 89101
(702) 382-8878

Riviera Hotel & Casino
Las Vegas, NV 89125
(702) 794-9233

Roadway Inn Suites Nellis
4288 North Nellis Boulevard, Las Vegas, NV 89115
(702) 632-0229

Royal Hotel & Casino
99 Convention Center Drive, Las Vegas, NV 89109
(702) 735-6117

Sam Boyds California Hotel & Casino
12 East Ogden Avenue, Las Vegas, NV 89101
(702) 385-1222

Sands Hotel Casino
3355 Las Vegas Boulevard South, Las Vegas, NV 89109
(702) 733-5000

Santa Fe Hotel & Casino
4949 North Rancho Drive, Las Vegas, NV 89130
(702) 658-4900

Silver Spur Hotel
1502 Las Vegas Boulevard South, Las Vegas, NV 89104
(702) 385-0809

Stardust Hotel & Casino
3000 Las Vegas Boulevard South, Las Vegas, NV 89109
(702) 732-6111
Sunrise Suites
4575 Boulder Highway, Las Vegas, NV 89121
(702) 434-0848

Sunrise Suites Hotel & Casino
4575 Boulder Highway, Las Vegas, NV 89121
(702) 948-8000

Texas Station Gambling Hall & Hotel
Las Vegas, NV 89101
(702) 631-1000

Thunderbird Hotel
1213 Las Vegas Boulevard South, Las Vegas, NV 89104
(702) 383-3100

Treasure Island at the Mirage
3300 Las Vegas Boulevard South, Las Vegas, NV 89109
(702) 894-7111

Tropicana Resort and Casino
Las Vegas, NV 89101
(702) 739-2222

Venetian Casino Resort
3355 Las Vegas Boulevard South, Las Vegas, NV
89109
(702) 733-5000

Victory Hotel Motel
307 South Main Street, Las Vegas, NV 89101
(702) 384-0260

Westward Ho Hotel & Casino
2900 Las Vegas Boulevard South, Las Vegas, NV
89109
(702) 731-2900

Fairfield Inn by Marriott
3850 Paradise Road, Las Vegas, NV 89109
(702) 791-0899

Fun City Motel
2233 Las Vegas Boulevard South Suite A, Las Vegas,
NV 89104
(702) 731-3155

Gold Spike Hotel & Casino
400 East Ogden Avenue, Las Vegas, NV 89101
(702) 384-8444

Wild Wild West Gambling Hall & Hotel
3330 West Tropicana Avenue, Las Vegas, NV 89103
(702) 740-0000

Royal Hotel & Casino
99 Convention Center Drive, Las Vegas, NV 89109
(702) 735-6117

El Morocco Hotel
2955 Las Vegas Boulevard South, Las Vegas, NV 89109
(702) 735-1255

Emerald Springs Holiday Inn
325 East Flamingo Road, Las Vegas, NV 89109
(702) 732-9100

Sahara Hotel (*high marks)
2535 Las Vegas Boulevard South, Las Vegas, NV
89109
(702) 737-2111

Daytona Beach, Florida

Adams Mark Daytona Beach Resort
100 North Atlantic Avenue, Daytona Beach, FL 32118
(407) 649-4945

Aladdin Inn Palace IN the Sun Restaurant
2323 South Atlantic Avenue, Daytona Beach, FL
32118
(904) 255-0476

Alpine Court Motel
518 South Atlantic Avenue, Daytona Beach, FL 32118
(904) 255-8558

Bayview Hotel
124 Orange Avenue, Daytona Beach, FL 32114
(904) 253-6844

Beach Quarters Inn
3711 South Atlantic Avenue, Daytona Beach, FL 32127
(904) 767-3119

Beacon by the Sea
1803 South Atlantic Avenue, Daytona Beach, FL 32118
(904) 255-3619

Bermuda Villas Motel
505 South Atlantic Avenue, Daytona Beach, FL 32118
(904) 255-2438

Camellia Motel
1055 North Atlantic Avenue, Daytona Beach, FL 32118
(904) 252-9963

Castaways Beach Resort
2043 South Atlantic Avenue, Daytona Beach, FL
32118
(904) 254-8480

Comfort Inn Oceanfront
3135 South Atlantic Avenue, Daytona Beach, FL
32118
(904) 767-8533

Cypress Cove
3245 South Atlantic Avenue, Daytona Beach, FL
32118
(904) 761-1660

Days Inn Oceanfront Central
1909 South Atlantic Avenue, Daytona Beach, FL
32118
(904) 255-4492

Daytona Beach Hilton Resort
2637 South Atlantic Avenue, Daytona Beach, FL
32118
(904) 767-7350

Fort Lauderdale, Florida

Bahama Hotel Deck
401 North Atlantic Boulevard, Fort Lauderdale, FL 33304
(954) 467-7315

Bahia Cabana Beach Resort
3001 Harbor Drive, Fort Lauderdale, FL 33316
(954) 524-1555

Beach Plaza Hotel
625 North Atlantic Boulevard, Fort Lauderdale, FL 33304
(954) 566-7631

Best Western FT Lauderdale Inn
1221 West State Road 84, Fort Lauderdale, FL 33315
(954) 462-7005

Captains Quarters Ocean Front Resort
4644 El Mar Drive, Fort Lauderdale, FL 33308
(954) 771-3919

Courtyard by Marriott
7780 Southwest 6th Street, Fort Lauderdale, FL 33324
(954) 475-1100

Courtyard by Marriott
7780 Southwest 6th Street, Fort Lauderdale, FL 33324
(954) 475-1100

Padre Island, Texas

Bahia Mar Resort
6300 Padre Boulevard, South Padre Island, TX 78597
(956) 761-1343
Best Western Fiesta Isles
5701 Padre Boulevard, South Padre Island, TX 78597
(956) 761-4913

Days Inn South Padre Island
3913 Padre Boulevard, South Padre Island, TX 78597
(956) 761-7831

Holiday Inn Sunspree Resort
100 Padre Boulevard, South Padre Island, TX 78597
(956) 761-5401

Miramar Resort Motel
1200 Padre Boulevard, South Padre Island, TX 78597
(956) 761-1100

Padre South Resort
1500 Gulf Boulevard, South Padre Island, TX 78597
(956) 761-4951

Ramada Limited
4109 Padre Boulevard, South Padre Island, TX 78597
(956) 761-4097

Sheraton Fiesta South Padre Island Beach Resort
310 Padre Boulevard, South Padre Island, TX 78597
(956) 761-6551

South Padre Motel
204 West Gardenia Street, South Padre Island, TX
78597
(956) 761-6701

TIKI the Condominium Hotel
South Padre Island, TX 78597
(956) 761-2694

Lake Havasu, Arizona

All Suite Hotel Sands Resort
2040 Mesquite Avenue, Lake Havasu City, AZ 86403
(520) 855-1388

Island Inn Hotel
1300 McCulloch Boulevard North, Lake Havasu City,
AZ 86403
(520) 680-0606

Lake Hills Inn
2781 Osborn Drive, Lake Havasu City, AZ 86406
(520) 505-5552

Ramada Inn
271 Lake Havasu Avenue South Suite 1, Lake Havasu City, AZ 86403
(520) 855-1111

Super 8 Motel
305 London Bridge Road, Lake Havasu City, AZ 86403
(520) 855-8844

Palm Springs, California

550 Warm Sands Hotel
550 South Warm Sands Drive, Palm Springs, CA 92264
(760) 320-7144

Abbey West Hotel
772 North Prescott Drive, Palm Springs, CA 92262
(760) 416-2654

Abbey West Hotel
772 North Prescott Drive, Palm Springs, CA 92262
(760) 416-2654

Avanti Resort
715 East San Lorenzo Road, Palm Springs, CA 92264
(760) 325-9723

Best Western Inn at Palm Springs
1633 South Palm Canyon Drive, Palm Springs, CA 92264
(760) 325-9177

Budget Host Inn
1277 South Palm Canyon Drive, Palm Springs, CA 92264
(760) 325-5574

Camp Palm Springs Mens Resort
1466 North Palm Canyon Drive, Palm Springs, CA 92262
(760) 322-2267

Canyon Club Hotel
960 North Palm Canyon Drive, Palm Springs, CA 92262
(760) 322-4367

Casa Cody Bed & Breakfast Country Inn
175 South Cahuilla Road, Palm Springs, CA 92262
(760) 320-9346

Columns Resort
537 South Grenfall Road, Palm Springs, CA 92264
(760) 325-0655

Coyote Inn
234 South Patencio Road, Palm Springs, CA 92262
(760) 327-0304

Desert House Inn
200 South Cahuilla Road, Palm Springs, CA 92262
(760) 325-5281

Desert Paradise Hotel
615 South Warm Sands Drive, Palm Springs, CA
92264
(760) 320-5650

Desert Riviera Hotel
610 East Palm Canyon Drive, Palm Springs, CA
92264
(760) 327-5314

Desert Shadows Inn
1533 North Chaparral Road, Palm Springs, CA 92262
(760) 325-6410

Desert Stars Resort
1491 South Viaduct Soledad, Palm Springs, CA
92264
(760) 325-2686

Hampton Inn
2000 North Palm Canyon Drive, Palm Springs, CA 92262
(760) 320-0555

Holiday Inn Palm Mountain Resort
155 South Belardo Road, Palm Springs, CA 92262
(760) 325-1301

Hotel California
424 East Palm Canyon Drive, Palm Springs, CA 92264
(760) 322-8855

Ingleside Inn
200 West Ramon Road, Palm Springs, CA 92264
(760) 325-0046

Inn of the 3 Palms
370 West Arenas Road, Palm Springs, CA 92262
(760) 323-2767

Intimate Resort
556 South Warm Sands Drive, Palm Springs, CA 92264
(760) 778-8334

Las Brisas Hotel
222 South Indian Canyon Drive, Palm Springs, CA 92262
(760) 325-4372

Le Palmier Inn
200 West Arenas Road, Palm Springs, CA 92262
(760) 320-8866

Morningside Inn
888 North Indian Canyon Drive, Palm Springs, CA 92262
(760) 325-2668

Mountain View Inn
200 South Cahuilla Road, Palm Springs, CA 92262
(760) 325-5281

Musicland Hotel
1342 South Palm Canyon Drive, Palm Springs, CA 92264
(760) 325-1326

Oasis Water Resort Villa Hotel
4190 East Palm Canyon Drive, Palm Springs, CA 92264
(760) 328-1499

Ocotillo Lodge
1111 East Palm Canyon Drive, Palm Springs, CA 92264
(760) 416-0678

Orchid Tree Inn
261 South Belardo Road, Palm Springs, CA 92262
(760) 325-2791

Palm Canyon Inn
1450 South Palm Canyon Drive, Palm Springs, CA
92264
(760) 320-7767

Palm Grove Hotel
2135 North Palm Canyon Drive, Palm Springs, CA
92262
(760) 323-4418

Peppertree Inn
645 North Indian Canyon Drive, Palm Springs, CA
92262
(760) 320-8774

Royal Sun Inn
1700 South Palm Canyon Drive, Palm Springs, CA
92264
(760) 327-1564

San Marino Hotel
225 West Baristo Road, Palm Springs, CA 92262
(760) 325-6902

Seven Springs Hotel
1269 East Palm Canyon Drive, Palm Springs, CA 92264
(760) 323-2775

Skye Jordan Inn
350 South Belardo Road, Palm Springs, CA 92262
(760) 325-2814

Smoke Tree Villa
1586 East Palm Canyon Drive, Palm Springs, CA 92264
(760) 323-2231

Vagabond Inn
1699 South Palm Canyon Drive, Palm Springs, CA 92264
(760) 325-7211

Federal listing for Best Banks for Small Business
The following lists by state:

ALASKA

First Bank
(907)228-4218

National Bank of Alaska
(907)267-5700

First Interstate Bank of Alaska
(800)688-2660

ALABAMA

Regions Bank
(205)290-5999

Union Planters Bank
(334)567-5141

Exchange Bank of Alabama
(205)274-2083

First National Bank of Central Alabama
(205)373-2922

West Alabama Bank & Trust
(205)375-6261

ARKANSAS

Regions Bank
(501)268-4211

Bank of Lincoln
(501)824-2265

Bank of Yellville
(870)449-4231

First National Bank of Mena
501)394-3552

Mercantile Bank of Arkansas
(501)688-1000

First National Bank of E. Arkansas
(870)633-3112

Commercial National Bank
(870)773-4561

ARIZONA

County Bank

(520)771-8100

Stockmens Bank
(520)757-7171

Bank One Arizona
(602)221-2900

Community Bank of Arizona
(520)684-7884

Bank of Casa Grande Valley
(520)836-4666

National Bank of Arizona
(520)571-1500

Mohave State Bank
(520)855-0000

<u>CALIFORNIA</u>

Mid-Peninsula Bank
(650)323-5150

WestAmerica Bank
(415)257-8057

International City Bank
(562)436-9800

Cupertino National Bank & Trust
(408)996-1144

Bank of America Community Development Bank
(626)453-8400

Mid-State Bank
(805)937-8551

Los Robles Bank
(805)373-6763

Wilshire State Bank
(213)387-3200

Butte Community Bank

(530)877-0857

Wells Fargo HSBC Trade Bank National
(415)396-6022

COLORADO

Norwest Pagosa
(970)264-4111

Castle Rock Bank
(303)688-5191

Canon National Bank
(719)473-8013

Bank of Grand Junction
(970)241-9000

Evergreen National Bank
(303)674-2700

Citizens State Bank of Ouray
(970)325-4478

Farmers State Bank of Calhan
(719)347-2727

Community First National Bank
(970)352-0077

First National Bank of Las Animas
(719)456-1512

Cheyenne Mountain Bank
(719)579-9150

Community First National Bank
(970)867-8281

CONNECTICUT

Equity Bank
(860)571-7200

New England Bank
(860)688-5251

Canaan National Bank
(860)824-5423

North American Bank & Trust
(203)377-0732

WASHINGTON D.C.

BB & T
(202)429-9888

First Liberty National Bank
(202)331-7031

Century National Bank
(202)496-4000

DELAWARE

County Bank
(302)226-9807

CHASE Manhattan Bank Delaware
(800)245-1032

Citibank Delaware
(302)323-3900

Bank of Delmarva N.A.
(302)629-2700

FLORIDA

Destin Bank
(850)837-8100

First Community Bank
(904)775-3115

Big Lake National Bank
(941)467-4663

Bank of Central Florida
(407)298-6600

First National Bank of Alachua
(904)462-1041

First National Bank of Wauchula
(941)773-4136

First National Bank of Crestview
(850)682-5111

Capital City Bank
(850)671-0300

First American Bank of Walton County
(850)267-0329

Farmers & Merchants Bank
(850)997-2591

Riverside National Bank of Florida
(561)466-1200

<u>GEORGIA</u>

Suntrust Bank
(404)588-7711

First State Bank
(770)474-7293

McIntosh State Bank
(770)775-9300

Lanier National Bank
(770)536-2265

Altamaha Bank & Trust
(912)594-6525

Cordele Banking Co.
(912)276-2400

First Bank of Coastal Georgia
(912)653-4396

First National Bank & Trust Co.
(912)552-9653

First National Bank of Chatsworth
(706)695-3201

Patterson Bank
(912)647-5332

HAWAII

Realty Finance Inc.
(808)961-0666

Hawaii National Bank
(808)528-7755

First Hawaiian Bank
(808)525-7000

IOWA

State Savings Bank
(712)523-2131

Farmers Savings Bank
(319)656-2265

Security Savings Bank
(515)448-5111

Racoon Valley State Bank
(515)993-4581

Peoples Bank & Trust Co.
(712)476-2746

Pilot Grove Savings Bank
(319)469-3951

Washington State Bank
(319)653-2151

Houghton State Bank
(712)623-4823

Security Bank
(319)382-9661

IDAHO

Pend Oreille Bank
(208)265-2232

Farmers National Bank
(208)543-4351

Panhandle State Bank
(208)263-0505

ILLINOIS

American Bank
(309)794-0111

National Bank
(217)532-3991

Holcomb State Bank
(815)393-4413

Town & Country Bank
(217)787-3100

State Bank of Geneva
(630)232-3200

National Bank of Petersburg
(217)632-3241

Germantown Trust & Savings Co.
(618)523-4050

Palmer American National Bank
(217)446-6450

Heritage Bank of Central Illinois
(309)362-2139

People's National Bank of Kewanee
(309)853-3333

Firstar Bank
(847)945-8550

Olney Trust Bank
(618)395-4311

Bank of Edwardsville
(618)656-0057

INDIANA

First State Bank
(812)443-4481

Citizens State Bank
(765)529-5450

Bank of Western Indiana
(765)793-4846

Frances Slocum Bank & Trust Co.
(219)563-4116

First Community Bank & Trust Co.
(317)422-5171

Community Bank of Southern Indiana
(812)944-2224

State Bank of Markle
(219)758-3111

KANSAS

The Peoples Bank
(316)672-5611

First Option Trust
(913)755-3811

First National Bank
(785)737-2311

First Community Bank & Trust Co.

(785)877-3313

First National Bank & Trust Co.
(785)543-6511

Emprise Bank
(316)383-4400

KENTUCKY

Eagle Bank
(606)824-4436

Farmers Bank
(502)756-5022

Bank of Columbia
(502)384-6433

Union Planters Bank
(502)441-1200

LOUSIANA

American Bank
(318)734-2226

Gulf Coast Bank
(318)893-7733

First Bank National
(318)783-4484

Community Trust Bank
(318)768-2531

MASSACHUSSETTS

Luzo Community Bank
(508)997-4555

Bank Boston National
(617)434-2200

Cape Cod Bank & Trust Co.
(508)790-4853

Bank of Western Massachusetts
(413)781-2265

Park West Bank & Trust Company

(413)747-1400

MARYLAND

Peninsula Bank
(410)651-2404

Saint Michaels Bank
(410)745-5091

First Bank of Frederick
(301)694-6464

Bank of the Eastern Shore
(410)228-5800

MAINE

United Bank
(207)942-5263

Katahdin Trust Company
(207)528-2211

Fleet Bank Maine

(207)874-5000

Union Trust Co.
(207)667-2504

MICHIGAN

CSB Bank
(810)395-4313

Shoreline Bank
(616)927-2251

Signature Bank
(517)269-9531

West Shore Bank
(616)757-4751

Bank of Lakeview
(517)352-7271

MINNESOTA

Village Bank

(612)753-3007

American Bank
(651)345-3311

Minnwest Bank
(507)283-9587

Marquette Bank
(612)797-8500

MISSOURI

Peoples Bank
(417)725-4191

Citizens Bank
(573)237-3051

First Bank
(314)567-4486

Nodaway Valley Bank
(660)562-3232

First Midwest Bank of Dexter

(573)624-3571

MISSISSIPPI

Lamar Bank
(601)794-8026

Mechanics Bank
(601)473-2261

Bank of Falkner
(601)837-9394

Hancock Bank
(228)868-4000

Bankplus
(601)247-1811

First Bank
(601)684-2231

MONTANA

Citizens Bank

(406)363-3551

Rocky Mountain Bank
(406)652-8877

Ruby Valley National Bank
(406)684-5678

NORTH CAROLINA

Bank of Currituck
(252)435-6331

Park Meridian Bank
(704)366-7275

Catawba Valley Bank
(828)431-2300

East Carolina Bank
(252)925-9461

NORTH DAKOTA

Page State Bank

(701)668-2261

Goose River Bank
(701)786-3110

First United Bank
(701)284-7810

Dakota Community Bank
(701)878-4416

NEBRASKA

Bank of Madison
(402)454-3381

Centennial Bank
(402)891-0003

Farmers State Bank
(402)782-3500

Hershey State Bank
(308)368-5555

First Nebraska Bank
(402)359-2281

Commercial State Bank
(402)586-2266

Farmers & Merchants Bank
(402)761-7600

Union Bank & Trust Co.
(402)483-9606

First National Bank in Ord
(308)728-3201

Platte Valley National Bank
(308)632-7004

First National Bank of Nebraska
(308)282-0050

Dakota County State Bank
(402)494-4215

Home State Bank
(402)234-2155

Adams Bank & Trust Co.
(308)284-4071

NEW HAMPSHIRE

First Colebrook Bank
(603)237-5551

Bank of New Hampshire
(603)624-6600

Granite Bank
(603)352-1600

First & Ocean National Bank
(603)474-5552

NEW JERSEY

Panasia Bank
(201)947-6666

Skylands Community Bank
(908)850-9010

Bank of Gloucester County
(609)845-0700

Union Center National Bank

(908)688-9500

NEW MEXICO

Peoples Bank
(505)758-4500

Bank of Belen
(505)865-2265

Ruidoso State Bank
(505)257-4043

Community First Bank
(505)527-6200

NEVADA

Comstock Bank
(775)824-7286

BankWest of Nevada
(702)248-4200

First National Bank of Ely

(702)289-4441

NEW YORK

Alliance Bank
(607)756-2831

Cho Hung Bank
(212)935-3500

Solvay Bank
(315)468-1661

Community Bank
(315)386-4553

Bath National Bank
(607)776-3381

OHIO

Savings Bank
(740)474-3191

Steel Valley Bank
(800)296-9910

OKLAHOMA

Landmark Bank (580)436-1117

OREGON

Columbia River Banking Co (541)298-6646

PENNSLYVANIA

PFC Bank (724)763-1221

SOUTH CAROLINA

Bank of Walterboro (843)549-2265

TENNESSEE

Citizens Bank (615)735-1490

TEXAS
First National Bank (940)696-3000

UTAH

Zions Fisrt National Bank (801)524-4690

Morgan Stanley Dean Witter Bank (801)566-4161

VIRGINIA
Virginia Bank & Trust Co (804)793-6411

WASHINGTON

Islanders Bank (360)378-2265

Adult Film Studios

If you would like to contact the larger studios for possible film work, below is the contact information to the three biggest. I highly recommend writing a simple short letter, versus calling, because it's a very strong chance your inquiry will be taken more serious. Here are the three addresses:

Vivid Video
15127 Califa Street
Van Nuys, CA 91411

Wicked Pictures
9040 Eton Avenue,
Canoga Park, CA 91304

Evil Angel Productions
14141 Covello St. 8C
Van Nuys, CA 91405

Have fun and let your delightful journey begin!
A *Very Special Wish*, Ray West

Proven handpicked resources to bring YOU maximum success

I personally guarantee it! -Ray

Catalog Number	Title	Paper Version	Software version at publisher list discount (pc/mac friendly)
Z-11	**How to Start Your Own Adult Website with 7 Bullet-Proof Strategies** - by top Studio Consultant, Dean Compton Drilling deep into 7 primary ways you can gain 300,000 visitors to *your* website, and **increase your profits up to 90% in the next three weeks...** proven strategies tightly wrap the **solutions you need.** (10 page exclusive)	$49.95	$29.95
Z-12	**How You Can Star and Direct Films for Adult Studios in the Next 6 Weeks!** - by Director James Creek Tested and proven "jaw-dropping" strategies you can use for gaining access to adult film sets. **How you can star with 100's of women in adult films within the next 6 weeks...** arming you with everything you need to know for *gaining* back stage access! (special guide 102 pages) *NEW!*	$114.95	$59.95
Z-13	**How to Market Your Own Adult Videos from the Internet and Skyrocket Your Profits Up to 50%** - by Director James Creek Gain 6 stealth marketing tactics to **increase your profits up to 50% from the Internet in the next 21 days...** armed with everything you need to know for gaining a stronghold on domestic and International adult markets from the comfort of your own home. (exclusive report 10 pages)	$49.95	$29.95
Z-14	**How You Can Find 60% More Female Talent for Your Adult Videos** -by top Studio Consultant, Dean Compton Discover how you can find up to **60% more female talent,** for your own adult films **in the next 3 days...** you'll discover not one new technique but 4 *Proven* strategies that will have **women calling you around the clock...** 6 out of 7 people are absolutely stunned by this information! (10 page exclusive) *NEW!*	$69.95	$39.95

* *Of course, results will vary, and aren't indicative of average performance.*

		Paper	Software
Z-15	**Your Genius at Work: How You Can Break the Bank by Selling Your Own Adult Content, and Increase Your Results by 5 Times!** by Director James Creek The product that **launched 1,000 successes,** while increasing profits up to 40%, and targeted results by five times... Reveals exactly what, how, when and why specific strategies work and how you can produce content people not only view - but respond to in droves. (exclusive report 9 pages)	$39.95	$19.95
Z-16	**How You Can Find Thousands of Affiliates for Your Adult Business and Increase Profits up to 97%** - by Producer Reese Lang This intense 3-section document will reveal **4 proven** strategies for overcoming the obstacles you're going to face with your own affiliate program. Discover how you can design and "mistake-proof" your business organization... with fast bullet-proof results! (special report 8 pages)	$39.95	$19.95
Z-17	**How to Write a Press Release for Millions of Untapped Market Potential** - by Producer Reese Lang How you can **double or even triple your customer base in 6 weeks** with FREE publicity... arming you with everything you need to know to produce the immediate **breakthroughs** *you* need. (exclusive report 6 pages)	$31.95	$14.95
Z-18	**How You Can Design and Produce Your Own Adult Video Catalog at 100% Profit Gain** - by top Studio Consultant, Dean Compton It's no secret. Adult mail order is a billion dollar market. This report **made Jacob Ross millions...** Discover how you can keep your finger on the pulse of the market as events unfold, and gain 100% profit growth in the next 30 days. Exclusive document could prove to be **the answer you're looking for.** (special report 10 pages)	$49.95	$29.95
Z-19	***Your* Own Blue Ribbon Adult Distributor List from Creek's Private Files** - by Director James Creek Any company can call themselves a distributor, but how many are real?... The Blue Ribbon distributor list represents the crème of the crop, with a publishing rating of 5 stars. In recent past, top professionals in the industry paid over $500 for this information... **Armed with these insider secrets,** you can easily produce your own integrated operating system, connect with more distributors, and **gain $47,000 in the next 3 months** from offering your own adult products... proven results give you everything you need to know to master the adult world market. (10 page exclusive) **NEW!**	$96.95	$49.95

* *Of course, results will vary, and aren't indicative of average performance.*

		Paper	Software
Z-20	**Your Secret Wealth: Adult Video Store, Chain Directory Version** - by top Studio Consultant, Dean Compton With over 200 secret listings, this private resource list is worth a fortune... you'll have **instant** access to move your videos into hundreds of stores nationwide the **same day** you receive the directory... **action based strategies you can take to the bank!** (12 page exclusive) **LIMITED QUANTITY!**	$104.95	$49.95
Z-21	*Your* Own Adult Video Producer and Director Contact List by Producer Reese Lang We are the only publishing company that has this **one-of-a-kind list.** Discover how you can personally contact the leading names in the adult industry... Little known information gives you key benefits for joint venturing breakthroughs, and producing **your own killer video deals - at 6 figure monetary levels.** (exclusive report 10 pages)	$69.95	$39.95
Z-22	**Increase Your Profit *Gain* Up to 40% with Your Own Adult Magazine and Newspaper Directory** - by Director James Creek Nothing is left out from this **one-of-a-kind** source. How you can locate adult magazine and newspaper editors... giving you little known secrets for *gaining* a combined print media audience of **9 million!** (special report 10 pages)	$67.95	$37.95
Z-23	**How You Can Gain FREE Instant Publicity from FM Radio Stations** - by Producer Reese Lang **Expect immediate results!** Everything you need to know for booking radio talk show appearances, and in some cases, giving *you* the ability to **make 5 to 6 phone interviews a week!**... INSTANT publicity proven to destroy the competition! (exclusive report 8 pages)	$47.95	$24.95
Z-24	**The Internet Search Engine Myth: Why They Are Unreliable to Make You Wealthy and What You Can Do About It!** - by top Studio Consultant Dean Compton Will search engines make you wealthy?... The revealing truth may shock you! After reading, **I'm sure you'll agree.** (one-of-a-kind report 10 pages)	$49.95	$29.95
Z-25	**Reese's Adult Wholesaler List** -by Producer Reese Lang A gentleman in Ohio made multi-millions by moving his adult products through wholesalers. Another made over a million... The *Reese List* will put you on every corner of the globe, with millions of potential new customers ready to buy your adult products... results proven to **increase your profit growth up to 96% in the next five months.** (9 page exclusive)	$49.95	$29.95

* *Of course, results will vary, and aren't indicative of average performance.*

ORDERING INFORMATION

Must be 18 years of age and legal in your community to order

If additional space is needed, you may duplicate this order form or list items on a separate piece of paper. Your order will receive immediate attention and will be **discreetly** shipped to you by the US Postal Service, and will arrive within 2 to 7 business days depending where you live.

*Free Secret Bonus - When you act now, your order will come with a **free 5-month** *Access Pass* to the online picture gallery ($60 value). You will have **free instant access to 9 eye-popping categories** with **over 200 mouth watering images...** your secret password, along with simple instructions, will be included with your package. If you do not have a computer, you'll have to use a friend's computer. (All parties must be at least 18 years of age and legal in the community from where the images are accessed).

The free 5-month *Access Pass* is easily worth the price of 4 hardcover books... its now yours absolutely **free.**

*Publisher Guarantee... **If for any reason your not making at least an extra $10,000 anytime within the next 365 days of purchase from using any of the material, simply return it for a full No Risk, No Questions Asked, Money Back Guarantee... Plus, for GIVING IT A TRY, you can still keep the free 5-month** *Access Pass* **to the online picture gallery.**

That's a 100% return on your investment - or it costs you nothing!... The only reason we can offer such a strong guarantee is because we're 100% confident you're going to fall in love with our down-to-earth strategies.

Quantity	Title	Order #	Format (software or paper version)	Price

Subtotal_____

Please add $2.00 Shipping & Handling for each software item, and $3.00 for each paper item.

TOTAL_____

☐ Check box for **email option.** You can have the software emailed to you... and **eliminate shipping and handling charges.** Please write your email address and make it easy to read. When your order arrives, your software will be attached and emailed to your address.

Email address _____

Again for error free purposes _____

The discount prices are subject to change anytime. Act now. All information that you enter is kept **confidential** and no record of your credit card is kept. We do not rent or sell our customer lists... **we respect your privacy.**

Can you afford to miss out?

Remember, **you have no risk.** You'll be armed with literally **everything you need** to turn your fantasy into a proven reality.

Don't put this off. The first version of wealth building packages sold out quickly and the second is expected to move just as fast.

There are 3 *easy* ways to order.

1) You can order online at http://www.rayscorner.com/access

2) Order by calling the office number at (804) 897-7250

3) You can fill in the order information below and send it to the address at the bottom of this page.

Method of Payment (please circle one)

(Visa) (Master Card) (American Express) (Discover) (Check/ Money Order)

Name as it appears on card _____

Account Number _____

Expiration Date _____

Signature (required for credit card orders) _____

Phone number or email address (double check email spelling)
_____

Please include your full shipping information below.

Name _____

Address _____

City or Town _____

State/ Province _____

Zip/ Postal _____